SPECIAL NEEDS IN ORDINARY SCHOOLS

General editor: Peter Mittler

Associate editors: Mel Ainscow, Brahm Norwich, Peter Pumfrey,
Rosemary Webb and Sheila Wolfendale

Change in Special Education

Titles in the Special Needs in Ordinary Schools series

Change in Special Education

What Brings it About?

Richard Stakes and Garry Hornby

CASSELL

Cassell
Wellington House   PO Box 605
125 Strand   Herndon
London WC2R 0BB   VA 20172

First published 1997

British Library Cataloguing-in-Publication Data
A catalogue record for this book is available from the British Library.

ISBN 0-304-33612-2 (hardback)
      0-304-33613-0 (paperback)

Typeset by Ruth Noble in Peebles, Scotland.
Printed and bound in Great Britain by Biddles Ltd, Guildford and King's Lynn.

Contents

Acknowledgement

The authors would like to thank all those who have contributed to this book.

Introduction

For over one hundred years, since the introduction of compulsory education, children with Special Educational Needs (SEN) have been educated in mainstream schools. In addition to educational considerations, the education provided for such pupils has been dependent on societal and political factors.

The purpose of this book is to analyse the factors that have been critical in influencing the development of provision for children with SEN in mainstream schools. Our analysis indicates that there are seven key determinants of the process of change. These factors can be best summarised as:

- political will to initiate and sustain developments with pupils with SEN
- adequacy of provision and resources to meet the needs of pupils with SEN
- societal attitudes to people with disabilities including children with SEN
- appropriateness of curricula to meet the needs of pupils with SEN
- the extent of integration of such pupils within mainstream schools
- the training of teachers regarding pupils with SEN
- the management of SEN provision in schools.

There is a long history of difficulties concerning the education of children with SEN in mainstream schools that can be traced back to the introduction of compulsory mainstream school education in the late nineteenth century. Our analysis indicates that these difficulties can be related to the above seven factors, specifically: a lack of political will; inadequate provision and resources; negative societal attitudes; inappropriate curricula disagreement over integration; inadequate teacher training and poor management of SEN provision.

Each of the seven factors plays its part in either facilitating or retarding change in the practice of special education in mainstream schools. Figure 1 illustrates an analogy that takes the form of a cartwheel. Each of the seven factors plays a part in determining progress. These can work individually or in harness with each other. For example, more positive societal attitudes towards those with disabilities can move practice forward. If such a move is coupled with political will and changes in legislation, the speed of progress will be enhanced.

Similarly, the cartwheel model can travel in reverse to reflect a deteriorating situation. An example of this might be where increased integration of children with SEN into mainstream schools with inappropriate curricula, leads to a deterioration in the education provided for them. When such a move is coupled with a change in resourcing policy from a demand-led model of funding of SEN provision to a resource-led model this would accelerate the reversal of progress.

Overall progress in SEN provision in mainstream schools is considered to be dependent on what is happening with each of the seven factors which have been identified. A combination of these factors is what determines whether the cartwheel of SEN provision rolls forward, remains static or moves backwards.

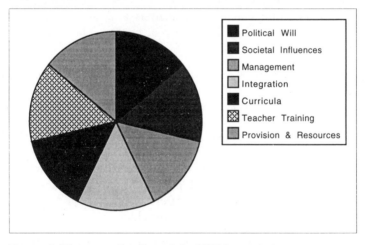

Figure 1: The cartwheel model of SEN provision

This book provides a historical analysis of the development of SEN provision in mainstream schools by focusing on the seven factors identified above. The book is intended to provoke further discussion of the issues which have been raised in order to increase awareness of the factors which influence change. It is hoped that this will lead to the development of increasingly effective provision for pupils with SEN in mainstream schools.

From Warnock to the Code of Practice

INTRODUCTION

It is just over one hundred years since provision for pupils with SEN was first made in mainstream schools. Currently such provision is at the forefront of debates about special education in the UK. The main reason for this is that there is a great deal of concern in mainstream education about the implementation of the recent Code of Practice for SEN (DfE 1994) which is the most far reaching guidance on SEN ever issued by the UK government.

Another reason that this topic is of considerable interest currently is that philosophical perspectives on special education have developed to a point where writers from various parts of the world are suggesting that separate SEN provision should not exist. For example, in the UK, Dyson (1990) proposed that, instead of specialist staff being employed to provide for pupils with SEN, schools should have 'effective learning consultants' who are concerned with optimising the learning of all pupils.

Likewise in the USA, proponents of the Regular Education Initiative, (e.g. Wang, Reynolds and Walberg 1988) have suggested that there is no need for a separate special education system. They argue that all pupils can be provided for in mainstream schools through teachers developing the skills and resources to teach children with SEN alongside other pupils. This is the same rationale which is repeatedly espoused by proponents of 'inclusive education', (e.g. Clark, Dyson and Millward 1995; Stainback and Stainback 1990) who believe that all children with SEN should, and can be, catered for within mainstream schools.

As a result, it appears that the wheel may be about to turn full circle for special education provision within mainstream schools. Progress can be traced from around the end of the last century when pupils with SEN were to be found in mainstream schools with no special provision made for them, through a period of almost one hundred years of the development of such provision, to a situation in which this may all be reversed in order to implement a model of full inclusion with little or no separate SEN provision.

However, government education policies over the past decade in the UK, and in several other countries with similar education systems, such as the USA and New Zealand, have created forces which have acted in opposition to this trend. The implementation of a prescriptive national curriculum, devolved budgets to schools, league tables of schools based on national assessment and examination results, an increase in selective schools and the rights of parents to choose schools for their children to attend, have all created a very different educational climate to that which spawned the inclusion philosophy just a few years ago. As Fish and Evans (1995, p. 109) suggest, 'special education is now being influenced by a new set of values, competition, choice and selection on merit – which inform policies for schools and colleges'.

In this new educational climate attitudes to pupils with SEN within mainstream schools have become less positive. Many schools consider that having a substantial number of pupils with SEN on the roll detracts from their performance in the examination league tables and therefore makes them less attractive to parents considering enrolling their children.

The field of special education is in a state of turmoil. This is not only the case in the UK but is also true in countries with a similar education system, as suggested in a recent article on special education in New Zealand (Mitchell 1996) and recent publications on special education in the USA (Henderson 1995; Kauffman and Hallahan 1995). This turmoil can be addressed through three key questions:

- How did special education get into such a mess?
- What factors are responsible for the current state of the field?
- What factors have brought about the changes in philosophy and approaches which have occurred which can help account for this over the last century?

It is considered that a greater understanding of the factors which have helped determine the current state of thinking and practice in the field of special education will help provide a better understanding of present circumstances as well as a clearer view of how the field should develop in the future.

These are the aims of this book. That is to elucidate the various factors responsible for bringing about change in special education so that a clearer vision of the future development of the field might be gained. This is clearly an important task but not an easy one. One danger of any attempted analysis of such a situation is that by imposing a structure in order to understand and analyse developments it is possible to introduce simplifications of complex sets of issues and circumstances. The authors realise this and therefore propose the following analysis with the intention that it will act as a catalyst to stimulate reflection and discussion, thereby promoting better understanding of the factors involved in bringing about change in special educational provision.

FACTORS INVOLVED IN BRINGING ABOUT CHANGE

One way to identify the various factors involved in bringing about change in special educational provision in mainstream schools is to reflect on how the recent Code of Practice (DfE 1994) came about and consider the various factors which will influence its implementation.

The Code of Practice consists of comprehensive guidance for schools and LEAs on how to implement the parts of the 1993 Education Act which are concerned with SEN. Such comprehensive guidance was necessary mainly because of growing concerns from the late 1980s onwards from parents, professional bodies and finally politicians, that the implementation of the 1981 Education Act, which put in place many of the recommendations of the Warnock Report (DES 1978) was becoming increasingly ineffective.

The results of two pieces of research, both conducted towards the end of the 1980s, contributed to a ground swell of opinion. A survey of LEAs on the implementation of the 1981 Act (Goacher, Evans, Welton and Wedell 1988) found that, although there had been a major shift in thinking about SEN, the effectiveness of provision was limited by an inadequacy of resources available to fully meet the needs of children with SEN. Similarly, a survey of secondary school provision which focused on the impact of the Warnock Report (Stakes 1990) found that, while attitudes within schools were more positive towards pupils with SEN, many of the recommended changes in SEN provision had not occurred.

In the early 1990s concerns about the effectiveness of SEN provision in mainstream schools was reinforced by the publication of the highly influential report 'Getting in on the Act' (DES 1992). This was extremely critical of the organisation of SEN provision in many schools and LEAs. The analysis of the situation documented in this report was supported by Mary Warnock herself by means of several television programmes and statements reported in the press during the period (e.g. Warnock 1992). Lady Warnock made it clear that the organisation of SEN provision in mainstream schools was not commensurate with the intentions of the Warnock Report and that, in her opinion, this was resulting in a situation in which the needs of many pupils with SEN were not being met.

The publication of the Warnock Report is generally considered to have been a turning point in the field of special education in the UK. The report endorsed the good practice which had been developed and laid out general principles for the organisation of SEN provision which are still regarded as applicable today. In many ways all the 1993 Act and the Code of Practice are intended to do is to ensure that these principles are implemented fully. The fact that this needed to be done suggests that there are certain factors which have militated against the full implementation of the intentions of the Warnock Report. If the Code of Practice is to be successful in bringing about the desired changes then these factors need to be identified and addressed.

From an analysis of events between the publication of the Warnock Report (DES 1978) and the 1993 Education Act it is possible to identify seven major interlinked factors which are implicated in the difficulties encountered in implementing the changes suggested in the Warnock Report. These are:

- a lack of political will to urge the required change
- insufficient allocation of resources to support these changes
- negative societal attitudes to the education of children with SEN
- a lack of agreement on appropriate curricula
- a divergence of views on integration
- changes in the organisation and availability of teacher training in the field of special education
- difficulties in the overall management of provision for SEN.

It is these factors which are the key determinants of change in SEN provision throughout this period. The influences of each of these factors with regard to the implementation of the recommendations of the Warnock Report are discussed below. Comments on their likely impact on the effectiveness of the Code of Practice in implementing the principles of the Report will also be made.

POLITICAL WILL

It is well known that it was Margaret Thatcher as Conservative Minister of Education who commissioned the Warnock Report in 1972. During the five years it took to produce the report there was considerable political turmoil in the UK, triggered by the economic crisis created by the massive increase in oil prices in 1975. In the year following the publication of the report in 1978 there was a change of government, with the Conservative Party regaining power with Margaret Thatcher as prime minister. Because she set up the Warnock Committee it might have been expected that she would be keen that its recommendations were taken up. However, in the meantime economic and political realities had changed.

In the period following the change of government in 1979 many of the recommendations contained in the Warnock Report were included in the 1981 Education Act which was entirely devoted to SEN. However, this Act was not actually implemented until 1 April 1983, almost five years after the Warnock Report was published. This delay leads one to question the level of political will or commitment towards the implementation of the recommendations of the committee which had been set up ten years earlier.

Further, some of the recommendations of the Warnock Report which required additional resourcing from the government, such as improvements in nursery education and the funding of research and curriculum development in SEN, were not implemented. Perhaps, then, it should be no surprise that the 1981 Act did not bring about many of the changes in SEN provision desired by the Warnock committee.

Similarly with the Code of Practice, the Government have made it clear that no additional money will be provided to schools or LEAs to implement its requirements, since it is considered that existing resources which schools are given to cater for pupils with SEN should be sufficient. This has prompted the suggestion that rather than an indication of the political will to bring about positive changes in SEN provision, the Code is in reality part of a cynical exercise by the Government to save money on children with SEN. This is to be achieved by placing more obligations on mainstream schools, therefore reducing the numbers of children obtaining statements of SEN and thereby expensive places in special schools.

ALLOCATION OF RESOURCES

There are three aspects of resourcing special educational needs which need to be considered: material, human and financial resources. Comments on material and financial resources will be made here while the topic of human resources will be addressed in the section on training.

The last 20 years have seen tremendous growth in the availability of material resources such as books, tests and computer equipment specifically designed for pupils with SEN. The emphasis in the Warnock Report on the estimate that one in five pupils will have SEN at some stage of their schooling probably contributed significantly to the interest of publishers and other organisations in producing materials for this population. While there is still room for improvement, the situation with regard to the availability of appropriate material resources for assessing and teaching children with SEN is now a quantum leap above where it was when the Warnock Committee began its deliberations.

In contrast, the picture regarding the allocation of financial resources is nowhere near as rosy. One of the main complaints from special educators about the Government's response to the Warnock Report was that insufficient funding was allocated to implement all of its major recommendations. This is considered to be a major factor behind the disappointing amount of progress achieved in some areas highlighted for change by the report.

Similarly with the Code of Practice, there have been limited additional resources set aside to ensure its effective implementation. Government ministers have been quoted as saying that the Code is 'cost neutral'. There has been a small amount of money available through GEST funding which has been used to provide training on the Code for Special Educational Needs Co-ordinators (SENCOs) but many people in the field consider that this is merely scratching the surface when it comes to working out a realistic costing for the effective implementation of the Code in schools.

The issue of resources reflects a shift which has occurred in the period between the publication of the Warnock Report and the introduction of the Code of Practice from a largely 'demand-led' concept of resourcing to one which is 'resource-led'. In the demand-led model of resourcing the financial resources required from the government are responsive to the requirements of the number of children who are deemed to have SEN. Therefore, an increase in the numbers of children identified in this way leads to an increase in government resources to meet this demand. Whereas, with the resource-led model, the funding allocated by the government is finite so that an increase in the number of children identified with SEN will lead to a decrease in the available funding for each of them. The analogy used by politicians for a resource-led model is of a cake which can be sliced in different ways but cannot be increased in size. The shift from demand-led to resource-led models of funding is one which has occurred across whole societies in Western countries and reflects one of the societal attitudes which need to be taken into account in discussing SEN provision.

SOCIETAL ATTITUDES

The shift from the demand-led to resource-led allocation of funding for SEN provision mentioned above is one which has acted in opposition to the implementation of the ideas of the Warnock Report, whereas other changes in societal attitudes have tended to support these ideas. Foremost of these are the views held by Western societies about the place of people with disabilities in these societies. During the 1970s and 1980s the trend towards the acceptance of the roles and rights of people with disabilities in society gained momentum. The Warnock Report itself not only reflected this trend but also contributed to it, with its emphasis on needs rather than categories of disability and with the belief that the majority of children with SEN should be educated in mainstream schools. As a result there appears to have been a corresponding change in the attitudes of teachers in schools towards pupils with SEN. In general, teachers in mainstream schools are now more positive about having children with various special needs in their classroom than they were twenty years ago (Stakes 1990).

A further societal change which has supported the implementation of the ideas in the Warnock Report is the increasing involvement of parents in the education of their children. This change has been accelerated by several education acts from 1980 to 1993 which have granted increased rights to all parents but particularly to those with children with SEN. The need for effective parental involvement was a key aspect of the recommendations in the Warnock Report and this has been supported by more positive societal attitudes and apparent political commitment (through, for example, the introduction of the Parents' Charter) to bring about such change.

The Code of Practice supports the changes noted above by focusing on these two areas in its list of five fundamental principles. It confirms that the need of most pupils with SEN will be best met in mainstream schools and places great importance on the need to work closely with parents. It therefore appears that the influence of societal attitudes is one factor involved in bringing about change in special education on which progress can clearly be seen during the last twenty years.

CURRICULUM ISSUES

The Warnock Report viewed curricular provision for pupils with SEN as needing to be determined by the overall aims of education for children with SEN. These, the report stated, were twofold.

Firstly, it was to enlarge children's knowledge of the world and secondly, to enable them to achieve as much independence as possible. This was a curriculum policy based on a liberal philosophy, with expectations of employment for many young people with SEN after school.

From an historical point of view this curriculum policy represented a radical change of emphasis from that which existed before the 1970s. Brennan (1979, 1985) suggested that, up to this point, curricular provision for children with SEN was largely inadequate and that much needed to be changed in order to fulfil the expectations created by the Warnock Report. Until the 1970s curricular provision for pupils with SEN was widely regarded as needing to be different from the mainstream curriculum. Therefore, specialist teachers in the field of SEN were given considerable licence in deciding the content of the curricula which they taught to pupils with SEN. However, in practice instead of a curriculum tailored specifically to meet their needs, many pupils with SEN in ordinary schools were exposed to a watered down mainstream curriculum along with relentless drill on basic literacy and numeracy skills.

The phased introduction of the National Curriculum (NC) in the latter part of the 1980s and the early 1990s had a major impact on curricular provision for pupils with SEN. For the first time since the beginning of the century a curriculum was specified and the freedom of teachers of pupils with SEN to determine such matters was ended. Unfortunately, the original National Curriculum was designed without any real consideration of the needs of pupils with SEN. In response to negative reactions from various parent and professional groups concerned with the education of such children the National Curriculum Council (NCC) quickly produced a document explaining its position on the place of pupils with SEN in the NC. This booklet, entitled 'A Curriculum for All' (NCC 1989) set out general guidelines on involving such pupils in the NC. It indicated that all pupils with SEN, including those with profound and multiple learning difficulties should follow the National Curriculum!

This document, and several others from the NCC which followed it, created considerable turmoil for teachers of children with learning difficulties. Many hours were spent and mental gymnastics undergone in order to rewrite the curricula of special schools for children with moderate and severe learning difficulties in terms of National Curriculum attainment targets. The problem was not so marked for teachers of children with mild learning difficulties. However, the overall impact was the same; to attempt to fit children into a rigid curriculum programme, rather than designing a curriculum to fit children's special educational needs.

The Code of Practice specifies the need for access to the full curriculum for all pupils with SEN. The philosophy behind this policy is that all children should have access to the full curriculum. In the past some groups of children had been denied the possibility of taking some subjects on the grounds of their disability. For example, some children with visual difficulties had been prevented from doing science and many children with physical difficulties had not been able to participate in physical education. The change to full curriculum entitlement for such children has been universally regarded as a positive feature of the introduction of the National Curriculum.

However, for the vast majority of children with SEN, who have varying degrees of learning difficulties, the imposition of the National Curriculum even with the increased flexibility allowed following the Dearing Report (Dearing 1994) has led to curricula which have been inappropriate for many. This issue has been complicated by moves within the field of special education towards the greater integration of pupils with SEN into mainstream schools, for which a common curriculum is a definite advantage.

INTEGRATION

The Warnock Report is often cited as being the source of the idea that wholesale integration of children with SEN into mainstream schools should be embarked upon. This is incorrect. The topic of integration had been debated at various times during the century but gained considerable momentum during the 1970s. The Warnock Report effectively side-stepped the debate regarding the advantages and disadvantages of the integration of children with SEN into mainstream schools. It simply re-affirmed the requirements of the 1976 Education Act, which encouraged such integration. This Act indicated that, subject to certain criteria, pupils with SEN should be educated in ordinary schools in preference to special schools. The four criteria were: that this was in accordance with parental wishes, that the child's educational needs could be met, that it was consistent with the efficient use of resources and that it would not detract from the education of the rest of the class.

However, despite the clear stipulations of these criteria in the 1981 Education Act many LEAs in the UK subsequently developed special education policies which involved progression towards a situation in which all children with SEN would be integrated into their local primary and secondary schools. On several occasions in the early 1990s Baroness Warnock made it clear that this was not the intention of the committee. She has consistently stated that, although the 1981 Act encouraged schools to integrate children with SEN, the committee recognised that there would always be a need for special schools (Warnock 1992).

In a series of studies Swann has investigated trends in the integration of children with SEN into mainstream schools. In his first survey, conducted in 1985 he found no evidence of increased levels of integration. In the second study, Swann (1991) found that between 1982 and 1990, there was a trend towards the increased integration of children with SEN into ordinary schools. However, in the most recent survey, covering the early 1990s, this trend has been reversed (DES 1996). Overall, his evidence indicates that since 1978 there has been a reduction from around 2 per cent to around 1.5 per cent in the proportion of pupils in special schools. Thus, it may be that the Warnock Report did have the impact on levels of integration which it desired. That is, it increased the proportion of pupils with SEN in mainstream schools while accepting that a small minority of children with SEN would need to continue being educated in special schools.

The stance taken in the Code of Practice on the integration issue is similar to that in the Warnock Report. The Code makes the point that the needs of most children with SEN can be met within mainstream schools whilst also emphasising the importance of having a continuum of SEN provision to meet a continuum of needs. The clear stance which the Code takes on the need for this continuum supports the philosophy on which the current range of SEN provision in most LEAs is based.

This appears to be particularly important at present, since many of the current changes in the practice of education in the UK, particularly as consequences of the 1988 Education Act seem to be working against the interest of many children with SEN who are integrated into ordinary schools. This is because current educational policy, which is based on economic competition and personal choice, is not compatible with the philosophy of integration (Fish and Evans 1995). Therefore, an urgent reappraisal of the entire issue of integration or inclusive education now seems imperative.

TEACHER TRAINING

The Warnock Report made wide-ranging recommendations regarding both initial teacher training and in-service training for teachers working with children with SEN. With regard to the initial training of teachers the Report has had an impact. A compulsory component on pupils with SEN has become a requirement of all courses relating to initial teacher training (ITT) in the UK. This has no doubt raised the profile of SEN work within ITT generally. However, since ITT courses have recently been required to be based in schools for at least two thirds of their time, the amount of attention devoted to this SEN component is generally considered to be inadequate to enable newly qualified teachers to be confident about identifying and teaching children with SEN in their classes (Garner 1996).

Further, in recent years there have been drastically reduced levels of funding available for the in-service training of teachers of children with SEN in the UK. As a result, many of the one-year full-time in-service courses in special education are being replaced by part-time modular courses, which are less costly (Miller and Garner 1996). While this change has spurned some innovative training pro-grammes (see Hornby 1990) it has also meant that most teachers are now expected to undergo INSET to prepare them to teach children with SEN in their own time and, increasingly, at their own expense. As a result the situation regarding teacher training in the SEN field in the mid-1990s is substantially worse than it was when the Warnock Report was published in 1978.

It is in this depressing climate that the Code of Practice was pub-lished in 1994. In order that schools can effectively implement the principles and practices espoused by the Code, training needs to be provided for several groups within the field of education. These include classroom teachers, teacher-aides and school governors. However, the greatest priority is for SENCOs to receive guidance on the requirements of the Code and about developing procedures to meet these within their own school. A small amount of money was provided through GEST funding, which has been used by most LEAs to provide brief training on the Code for SENCOs but there is no additional money available to meet their ongoing training needs or the needs of the other groups mentioned above.

MANAGEMENT

One of the key principles of the Warnock Report regarding the man-agement of SEN provision was that the school should adopt whole-school approaches to meeting SEN. This was in contrast to the ways in which schools had typically compartmentalised special education-al provision up to that time. Pupils with SEN were viewed as those children who were taught in special classes or special schools by teachers trained in special education. The Warnock Report empha-sised the estimate that one in five pupils will have SEN at some stage of their school career. Therefore, all teachers are likely to have pupils with SEN in their classes. This means that all teachers need to be knowledgeable about teaching children with SEN. It also means that there have to be school-wide procedures for identifying, assessing and helping pupils with SEN.

The success of the Warnock Report in publicising the need for a whole-school approach to SEN can be seen in the large number of books and courses on special education which appeared in the 1980s which used this phrase in their title (e.g. Dean 1989). In practice, the movement of schools towards whole-school approaches appears to have been evolving slowly.

The management of the recommendations contained in the Warnock Report and the subsequent Education Act (1981) has been largely inconsistent and has led to patchy provision throughout the country. The level of dissatisfaction about the extent of this can be gauged by the fact that a major aim of the Code of Practice (1994) appears to be to ensure that all schools adopt an effective whole-school approach. The fact that the title of the Code includes 'identification and assessment' of SEN and that its major thrust is a five stage approach for meeting SEN within schools, suggests that it was considered by the DfE that clear guidance was needed by many schools and LEAs in order to effectively implement whole-school approaches for managing their SEN provision.

The Warnock Report and the 1981 Education Act highlighted a number of important management issues. These included: the management of statements of special educational need, the financing of resources and budgeting arrangements specifically for pupils with SEN.

Statements of special educational need were originally intended to be used with approximately 2 per cent of pupils with the most severe disabilities, who at the time of the 1981 Education Act were segregated in special schools. However, since the implementation of statementing in 1983, there has been a drift of many of these pupils into mainstream schools as part of the movement towards greater integration. The statementing process has been increasingly seen as beneficial to other pupils who, before the Warnock Report, would never even have been considered for special school placement. The largest group of such pupils are those with specific learning difficulties whose parents have been influential in attempting to obtain a higher level of resources to meet their children's SEN.

The current situation is one where the proportion of children with statements of SEN is nearer to 3 per cent than the 2 per cent indicated earlier (Pyke 1996). Approximately half of these pupils are in mainstream schools. What is more, the number of requests for formal assessments leading to statements and appeals lodged by parents whose children were refused a statement by an LEA increased dramatically in the early 1990s.

The problem has been that since the introduction of the statementing process, parents of children with SEN began to see that the only effective way to ensure that their children would get additional resources to meet their needs was through this procedure. This is an understandable consequence of the move to a resource-led model of funding special education. The resulting situation reached in the early 1990s was one on which Baroness Warnock (1993, p. ix) commented 'It is generally agreed that the issuing of statements by LEAs has fallen into disarray.' She went on to suggest that since statementing was clearly not now achieving the purpose for which it was intended it should be abolished! In the event, rather than abolishing statementing the DfE has produced the Code of Practice, presumably with the intention that by ensuring schools follow the five-stage procedures the number of statemented children will be reduced.

The Audit Commission Report (DES 1992) indicated that there has been little accountability for the portion of the schools' budget provided by the LEA specifically for SEN. Further, they indicated that in the past there has not only been a lack of awareness of how resources have been allocated but also a lack of accountability over their use and an evaluation of their effectiveness in achieving satisfactory pupil progress. It will be interesting to see how the implementation of the Code, Circular 6/94 and regular OFSTED inspections will change the situation. The intention of this new guidance is that from now on schools will need to identify specific spending on SEN from the overall school budget. Schools will also have to justify the allocation of resources, financial, human and material to different aspects of their provision for SEN.

CONCLUSIONS

It is argued in this book that the seven factors discussed in this chapter have had a major impact on the provision made for children with SEN throughout the whole period of compulsory education in the UK. In the following chapters the impact of each of these seven factors in determining change in SEN provision in mainstream schools over the past hundred years will be considered.

Political will

INTRODUCTION

Among the most important influences affecting changes in provision made for children with SEN have been political factors. In some circumstances debates that have occurred in society have led to pressure for legislative changes. In this respect Parliament has been a major focus for change in SEN provision. Parliamentary debates reflect highly complex issues, relating to the changing attitudes within society towards children with SEN, as well as to the pace and direction of changes initiated by the legislation.

It is the purpose of this chapter to discuss the main changes in legislation which have affected pupils with SEN, their parents and teachers throughout the period of compulsory schooling in England and Wales. Additionally, through an analysis of the effects of this legislation, attention will be focused on the tensions involved and to the general lack of direction of government policy regarding pupils with SEN.

THE SYSTEM OF GOVERNMENT

Government legislation and guidance affecting provision for children with SEN since the last century has been both of a general and a specific nature. General legislation, for the purposes of this chapter, refers to the legislation enacted by Parliament which affects the education of all children regardless of their need for special educational provision. There have been many examples of this since the introduction of compulsory schooling. The most important recent example is the introduction of the National Curriculum in the 1988 Education Act. Specific legislation and guidance is defined as that which is directly concerned with children with SEN. There have been fewer initiatives of this type during the same period. The most recent example included the Education Act (1981) and the introduction of the Code of Practice (DES 1994) accompanying the 1993 Education Act. This chapter will provide an overview of both general and specific legislation affecting provision for pupils with SEN in mainstream schools but the main emphasis will be on specific government initiatives affecting strategy.

The advisory nature of much of the legislation that has been enacted has led to widely different interpretations throughout the country. It is the central theme of this chapter that this legislation has generally been brought about by consistent pressures exerted by individuals and groups at both national and local government level. Much of what has been achieved has been dependent on the work of enthusiastic and committed individuals.

Change in the legislation affecting pupils with SEN, as with any other legislation, has to take into account the parliamentary system of government in the UK. This is regarded as the cornerstone of change in a democratic society. Changes which are brought about are dependent on what is commonly described as 'the will of Parliament'. This concept is an important overarching feature which can be closely related to the context, tone and direction of national policy-making for children in school with SEN.

Educational provision for pupils with SEN throughout the period of compulsory education in England and Wales has reflected contemporary political thinking. The legislation to protect, let alone enhance, the educational prospects of children with SEN has often been inconsistent and divisive. Further, the implementation of the legislation has often been under-resourced and at times of economic difficulty it has been among the first in line for cutbacks.

THE PREVALENCE OF CHILDREN WITH SEN

At the outset of compulsory education there was little knowledge of the number of pupils with disabilities and learning difficulties. Before the introduction of compulsory schooling towards the end of the nineteenth century provision for pupils with SEN was largely on an ad hoc basis. The evidence from Pritchard (1963), Hurt (1988), Cole (1989) and Sutherland (1971) indicated that where special provision did exist it was most likely to be made for pupils who were blind or deaf.

Even when attendance at elementary school was made compulsory in 1880 there was no knowledge of the actual numbers of children in the country who would be in need of SEN provision. Indeed, it is likely that many children who would now be classified as having SEN continued not to attend school and were put to work doing menial tasks or were incarcerated in workhouses or asylums. To some extent this is reflected in the school attendance figures. Ellis (1973) indicated that in 1880 the number of children registered in elementary schools was 3.8 million. This had increased to 5.7 million in 1900. This represented an increase from 74 per cent of children registered at the introduction of compulsory schooling to 88 per cent at the turn of the century.

A further problem was that of the payment that was necessary in order for children to attend school. This feature was not removed until 1891, and one which Hurt (1988) indicated was a key factor in non-attendance for some able-bodied children, let alone those with disabilities or learning difficulties. For working class parents, who were already living on or about the poverty line, school attendance was an added financial burden.

Such families saw compulsory education as an imposition which disrupted family life and exacerbated their poor social conditions. Evidence provided by Humphries and Gordon (1992) and Hurt (1988) indicated that even beyond the First World War many working class parents of children with SEN did their best to ignore the attendance requirements and kept their children at home.

The first estimate of the number of pupils with SEN in schools came through the work of doctors in the late nineteenth century. There were wide variations in the estimates that were made. Warner, the Chief Medical Officer of Health for London in 1896 estimated that only 1 per cent of the capital's children needed extra help to aid their educational development. As a contrast, and much more in line with contemporary thinking, also in 1896 Crichton-Browne (quoted in Lumsden 1968) was reported as suggesting that in London some 20 per cent of pupils attending schools were 'backward'.

Despite the work of various reports and Royal Commissions, there was little recorded improvement in the overall knowledge of the number of pupils with learning difficulties or other disabilities until after the First World War. One contributory factor to this was the financial implications for governments of finding that there was a large proportion of the school population with SEN.

THE EGERTON COMMITTEE (1889)

The Egerton Committee (1889) was the first attempt by national government to investigate the best way of fulfilling the educational needs of pupils with SEN in schools. The Government, however, could take little credit for its commissioning, since it was inaugurated in response to extreme pressure from outside Parliament, through organised groups and influential individuals working mainly with the 'blind' and the 'deaf and dumb'. There was a widespread belief that the educational and social needs of these children were not being met. Unlike other areas of disability at this time these pressure groups were well co-ordinated. Nevertheless, Pritchard (1963) and Cole (1989) indicated that it took considerable and concerted pressure from such groups before the Committee was initiated.

Despite considerable pressure, particularly from teachers, elementary schools were not included in the terms of reference of the Egerton Committee. As such, little evidence was collected about their educational needs, and as a consequence little was done in any co-ordinated way to help them. However, two important pointers for future developments in this area emerged from the work of this Committee.

Firstly, the recommendations of the Committee reflected both the overarching humanitarian and moral views of contemporary Victorian society. Some of these values were based on contemporary humanitarian and moral thinking, while others were based on misinformation and inaccurate medical knowledge.

The second issue related to the financing of the recommendations of the report. Any major changes would be costly to implement because they would require a long-term commitment. Further, to spend money on pupils with some types of disability was contentious to a large group of MPs, who had varying degrees of interest and sympathy for them. For children with learning difficulties this was a particular difficulty. Many people across a broad stratum of society at this time saw there was little value in investing in such children as many of them were regarded as lazy and of little real worth.

EDUCATION ACT (1893)

The recommendations made by the Egerton Committee (1889) were generally well received by those working in the areas of special education concerned with the blind and the deaf. However, the Education Act (1893) which followed solved few of the problems facing pupils with SEN, or their teachers. This was the case partially because the Act had not been directed at those with other than sensory difficulties and also because of difficulties over financing the recommendations. The lack of an overall commitment made by many MPs was evident in that the requirements of the Act were not made mandatory on School Boards. Because of this the main outcome of the Act was to increase pressure on the Government to do more for groups of children with SEN other than sensory difficulties.

These pressures were directed at the Government from a variety of sources. A pamphlet published by the Charities Organisation (COS) in 1893 demanded the provision of meaningful education for all children, whatever their level of ability. In 1896 the newly formed Society for the Promotion of the Welfare of the Feeble-Minded attempted to influence the Ministry of Education to widen the scope of the 1893 Act. So little had been done by some School Boards that Lord Egerton, in a manner similar to that of Lady Warnock in the 1990s, felt it necessary to re-involve himself in the debate. He attempted to change national apathy and called for an extension of the Act to widen the scope of provision.

One of the places where something was achieved for pupils with SEN as a result of the Egerton Committee was in London. Here, ideas were more advanced than in other parts of the country and, also, there were a larger number of children who needed help. Pressure was generated by the London School Boards who wanted two major developments of provision. These were bigger grants for children with SEN (these had been fixed at infant school level for all children with SEN) and the extension of the school leaving age for all in this group to 16 years. It was argued that such an approach would better prepare children with SEN for adult life. However, both of these suggestions were met with considerable scepticism by the Government. It was concerned on the one hand about costs and on the other about the degree of shift in the control that such a move might have.

THE SHARPE COMMITTEE (1898)

During the 1890s pressure for change from concerned organisations, teachers and members of the medical profession continued to build and eventually a further committee of inquiry was initiated by the Government. The Sharpe Committee reported in 1898 after sitting for about 15 months. They visited every special school in the country and collected evidence from a wide range of interested parties and professionals. These included a range of people representing teachers, doctors, educational inspectors, administrators and representatives from the welfare services.

Despite receiving much conflicting evidence, the Committee made a number of recommendations. These included: changes in the descriptive terms used for pupils with disabilities at that time, the role of the School Boards, the age of referral for extra help and the role of the medical profession in the process as well as considerations of the effect of peer attitude on children with SEN.

The terminology used to describe children with SEN was revised and updated. The use of the term defective, it was argued, should be used as an umbrella term for all children who were either physically or mentally disabled and who were not able to receive an education in mainstream schools. The term feeble-minded was considered to be no longer acceptable and was dropped from the terminology.

The Sharpe Committee recommended that local School Boards should be required to provide special classes for all educable children in their area. The definition of educable caused some difficulties for the Committee. Eventually they reached a working definition that for a child at school the teacher should have a major role to play in deciding this, for a child at home it should be the doctor who had this responsibility.

As for the age of referral, the view was taken that this should not occur before the age of seven. It was argued that until then lack of progress could be accounted for by a developmental delay and progress could occur at an accelerated rate later. The need for outside professional involvement was also noted. It recommended that Medical Officers should be appointed on a part-time basis to work on examining children.

The consequences of peer attitudes were also addressed. The Committee recommended that, wherever possible, special schools should be set up rather than special classes in ordinary schools. They felt this approach would avoid pupils with SEN being teased and harassed by their more able peers. However, the Committee were so impressed by the attitude and progress of pupils who had already been placed in special classes they indicated that special schools should only be built in towns where the population was over 20 000 people.

THE EDUCATION ACT (1899)

Some of the recommendations of the Sharpe Committee were incorporated into the Education Act (1899). As with the 1893 Act, the Government had certain difficulties in convincing its own supporters of its value. This is reflected in both the tone of the wording of the Bill and the clear emphasis on its financial implications.

To accommodate the difficulties encountered at the time of the previous Act, the 1899 Act again empowered rather than required school authorities to make provision. It was left up to local School Boards to decide on the amount of provision. This, despite the recommendations of the Committee, could be either in separate schools or in special classes in elementary schools. The Act also required that all children needing special help were to remain at school until the age of sixteen. The Act also empowered authorities to assess children whom it was considered were mentally defective or epileptic.

The consequence of this approach was that change was patchy as implementation was left to local government. In 1910 the Chief Medical Officer to the Board of Education indicated that fewer than half of the local authorities had made any attempt at provision for pupils with SEN.

There has been some disagreement as to the impact of the 1899 Act. Potts (1982a) argued that the situation stagnated because of an overall lack of political will by the Government. However, both Ingram (1958) and Tansley and Gulliford (1960) considered that the evidence from school log books shows that much was being done at an individual level by teachers themselves and the period was one in which there was growing provision for pupils with SEN. The nature of the language and general thrust of the 1899 Act meant that progress was largely dependent on the individual school or local education authority. This occurred despite the lack of overall strategy or commitment at a national level.

THE ROYAL COMMISSION (1908)

The impact of the Education Acts of 1893 and 1899 at local level was both confusing and piecemeal, serving only to frustrate both parents and teachers. This led to continued pressure for a further enquiry. This was agreed and the Royal Commission, chaired by Lord Radnor, subsequently sat from 1904 to 1908 in an attempt to regularise provision and to calm the situation.

The Royal Commission took a considerable amount of evidence from a wide range of interested professionals. However, much of this evidence only re-hashed the ongoing debate from the previous committees. In particular, the issues were related to the origins of the problems exhibited by many children which prevented them from taking full advantage of the education offered to them and to the continuing dilemma of deciding the best way of dealing with them.

There was considerable disagreement between the members of the Commission on the origins of the difficulties of children with SEN. This debate related to the relationship between the nature of children and the approach to their nurturing. It was clear at the time that many of the children with learning difficulties in mainstream schools had origins in the working class. It was they who had the greatest difficulty in settling to the demands of school and benefiting from the experience. Further, at that time middle class families were more likely to hide or at least attempt to disguise children who had difficulties (Humphries and Gordon 1992). Further, they pointed out that such children of the middle or upper classes would more often be provided for privately. For those children who could be seen as having more environmentally based difficulties, such as the conditions at home or the area they lived in, the Commission recommended the continuance of special classes in ordinary schools.

To the dismay of many, the Royal Commission continued to advocate the development of separate provision for many pupils whose educational difficulties were described as of a genetic origin and who were currently being taught in separate classes. The Commission considered that these pupils would best be served by community style provision, often in a rural setting. This move was seen by Tomlinson (1982) as aimed at persuading the higher social classes to see these schools as a distinct form of provision for their feeble-minded children.

As far as developing provision was concerned, little of any value came from the work of this Commission. Rather, the evidence collected highlighted the high level of confusion that existed regarding the development of policy and the considerable diversity of opinions among the professionals involved.

THE EDUCATION ACT (1913)

Some progress in terms of overall thinking on provision occurred during the period after the Commission's report. This was reflected in the provisions set out in the 1913 Education Act. After the largely recommendatory approach of the two previous Acts in 1893 and 1899, this Act (the Defective and Epileptic Children's Act) made it the statutory duty of every Local Education Authority to establish provision for all children who were categorised as having disabilities. The only exceptions made were for those in the lowest grade of feeble-mindedness.

Pressure brought to bear on Parliament had emphasised the need for developing a uniform national system of provision for children with SEN. This would have resulted in real change and an opportunity for a greater uniformity of provision. In the event however, this Act was not implemented. This had nothing to do with the will of Parliament on this occasion. The date set for implementation was 1 August 1914 and the Act was lost in the wider issues brought about by the outbreak of the First World War in Europe. Any changes in

SEN provision had to wait until after the war had finished.

Overall, the period before the outbreak of the First World War cannot be considered a success as far as the development of provision for children with SEN was concerned. The Commissions and Committees which considered SEN provision had produced little of a coherent policy and much of what progress there had been was piecemeal. Although there had been developments during the period, and governments had made some attempts to assess the need for provision, an overall lack of commitment, as well as worries over the financing of measures proposed, left England and Wales with less than adequate provision. Perhaps the position was best summed up by Fox (1918, p. 17) as one of 'inactivity, confusion and uncertainty'.

The issues raised prior to the start of the First World War remained to be tackled after it had finished in 1918. The difficulties in doing so had increased rather than diminished. This can be attributed to a number of factors. These included the overall war weariness that blanketed the country in the early 1920s, compounded by the effects of the number of deaths that had occurred as a consequence of the hostilities. Further, the overall national economic situation was weak and any improvements and changes to the system of education had to be carefully financed from an already difficult funding base. As a consequence, although the need for extra resourcing for SEN was a considerable concern for both classroom teachers and parents, it continued to have a low priority on the national educational agenda. As well as these socio-economic factors, the Eugenicists had a considerable influence in the inter-war years, with their views on separation and sterilisation of people with disabilities. Their views as well as a general lack of knowledge from all of the professional groups involved did not aid the process of change.

THE EDUCATION ACT (1921)

One focus of the 1921 Education Act was an attempt to address improvements in provision for pupils with SEN. Despite the call for a more enlightened, co-ordinated national provision the 1921 Education Act reflected the continuing influence of those who had supported separation at the beginning of the century. It was an influence which Tomlinson (1982) indicates was to last throughout much of the next ten years.

The 1921 Act defined more closely the various levels of learning difficulty and linked this with appropriate provision. Three categories of learning difficulties were detailed. These were: the imbecile, the defective and the dull or backward child. Separate provision was required by the 1921 Education Act for all children which it defined as imbecile. Children classified as imbeciles were regarded as ineducable and, in line with previous policy, did not feature as part of the provision of the Department of Education but rather the Department of Health. The education of these children was to be conducted entirely separately outside the school service.

Defective children were required to be educated in a special school or in a special class in a mainstream school. These children also had to be certified as being in need of this provision by the school's medical officer of health. Dull or backward children were generally regarded as being educable in the mainstream school. This latter category of children formed the largest of the three groups identified in the Act. They often appeared as the least capable children in the mainstream school classes they attended.

THE WOOD REPORT (1929)

The effect of the 1921 Act on SEN provision was largely negative. Its elementary system of classification, and the certification of pupils in special schools left major difficulties for both the children and their parents who resented its social and educational implications. A further difficulty was the continuing lack of knowledge of the number of pupils who needed SEN help. As a result of these difficulties a further committee of enquiry was set up.

The Wood Committee reported in 1929. One of its key duties was to determine the number of pupils with SEN. This was necessary in order to prevent local authorities having to continue to rely on guesswork. Such a move would also allow for a better understanding of the financial outlay which was required to meet the needs of these pupils. A concurrent survey to the Wood Committee indicated that some 10 per cent of children had special needs. These children formed the largest proportion of the three groups of children detailed in the 1921 Education Act.

The Wood Committee clearly took into account the opinions of many who had given evidence to it. Essentially, the recommendations it made were positive, pragmatic and attempted to alleviate some of the problems caused by previous legislation. The Committee took into account the changing attitudes in society in recommending that the categories of children described as retarded or feeble-minded should be abolished. It was considered that there was a growing stigma attached to these labels and that abolition would help to undermine this.

The discontinuance of all-age special classes in schools was also recommended. The Committee also questioned the level of IQ of those regarded as ineducable. It asserted that many more children were capable of receiving instruction in mainstream schools than was then the case. Further, it was felt that children with an IQ of less than 50 would gain, at least socially, from mainstreaming.

There were, however, clearly different views about opportunities for children with difficulties in the two phases of education. The overall view of the Committee was that the primary school would be much more likely to provide a better environment for children with SEN than the secondary school. In the circumstances this was hardly surprising. The secondary school at the time was based on a restricted, even socially elitist, entry and was strongly subject centred compared with its primary counterpart.

It was the view of Tomlinson (1982) that the Wood Report attempted to present special education as a helpful variation of mainstream education. Equally, it served to confuse the policy-makers. Although the main thrust of the Report attempted to lessen the stigma attached to special schools, at the same time it recommended an expansion of this form of provision in the urban areas.

However, its publication again coincided with national economic difficulties. Economic difficulties in the early 1920s had already seen tightening of the money provided for education and a 1927 circular advised of the imprudence of incurring extra expenditure on new schools for pupils with SEN. 1929 was the start of the 'great economic depression' which affected the whole world throughout the next decade. The timing of publication of the Wood Report (1929) ensured virtual inaction resulted.

It was not just problems relating to the national finances which served to undermine the recommendations of the Wood Report. The DES (1964) suggested that the Committee helped to paralyse action by its own comments on the scale of the problems. Further, it argued that by indicating there were a number of major problems in a variety of areas, the Report served rather as a marker for future action than a catalyst for contemporary change. Significantly, the same DES document summed up the inter-war years, as far as the education of those with SEN was concerned, as a period where although there were no real advances, it was a time of consolidation during which considerable progress was made! Much of this consolidation was not of a political nature, rather it was taking place in classrooms through the development of greater expertise of teachers and other professionals in the field. It was a time of advancement in the field of assessment, particularly formal testing, and in the area of child health.

Evidence of this wider understanding emerged in Government

funded reports, such as the Hadow Report (HMSO 1926) and the Spens Report (HMSO 1938). These reports reflected the growing belief that as many children with SEN as possible should receive their education in mainstream schools. This was a philosophy which would be carried through to the legislation of the 1944 Education Act.

THE EDUCATION ACT (1944)

The immediate post-war period has been described by social historians such as Marwick (1968), Calvocoressi (1978) and Hennessy (1992) as a time of optimism and change in Britain. Lawson and Silver (1973) indicated that, in educational terms, it was the time of radically reappraising education. The legislation incorporated in the 1944 Education Act initially reflected these aspirations.

The philosophy and direction behind the 1944 Act was clear from previous in documentation such as the Hadow Report (HMSO 1926) and Spens Report (HMSO 1938) the White Paper (HMSO 1943) and the Green Paper (HMSO 1943).

As far as children with SEN were concerned, examples of changing attitudes appeared in the White Paper on Educational Reconstruction (HMSO 1943). It concluded that there was a need for substantial modifications to current legislation. The Green Paper entitled *Education After the War* (HMSO 1943) indicated that, for most children with SEN, provision should be made within the ordinary school. In the light of the difficulties encountered as a result of the 1921 Act, particularly the general dislike of the system of certification, a radical reappraisal of SEN was thought to be needed. Pressure was exerted to provide a more inclusive approach to provision.

This point was emphasised by Chuter Ede (Hansard 1944) as Secretary to the Board of Education when the Bill was passing through Parliament. He indicated that the Government did not want to insert any words into the Bill that would make it appear that the usual way to deal with a child with SEN was placement in a segregated special school.

Provision for children with SEN was an important aspect of the 1944 Act. Children with SEN were to be placed in one of eleven categories of handicap: blind, partially sighted, deaf, partially deaf, epileptic, educationally sub-normal, maladjusted, physically handicapped, speech defective, delicate and diabetic. The 1944 Act required that LEAs had to ascertain the needs of children in their area for special educational treatment. It indicated that this should be undertaken in mainstream schools wherever possible. The 1944 Act also introduced the tripartite system of secondary education, with grammar, technical and modern schools. The majority of pupils needing special educational treatment attended secondary modern schools.

In reality the implementation of the 1944 Act did not match its aspirations. This was particularly the case in the secondary school. Over the next twenty years the tripartite system of secondary provision was seen as divisive and largely discredited. The pressure for change was growing, not only from those with interests in children with SEN but also from many others who felt the situation to be unjust and failing many pupils. By the early 1960s there were attempts by individuals such as Pedley (1969) to change the system of secondary school provision.

THE NEWSOM REPORT (1963)

The Newsom Report (1963) on secondary modern schools, which most children with SEN attended, provided little hard evidence about the amount of provision available for pupils with SEN. However, it did suggest that there were serious gaps and what was available was largely dependent on attitudes within individual schools, particularly the views of the head teacher. The report indicated that where provision had been made some 10 to 15 per cent of the school population were regarded as having SEN.

There is conflicting evidence with regard to the amount of SEN provision that was available by the end of the decade. Sampson and Pumfrey (1970) indicated that SEN provision was widespread throughout the secondary sector. However, the DES (1971) reported that only one third of secondary schools made any provision for pupils who required special help because of their learning problems. No mention was made in this report of pupils with physical or sensory disabilities receiving help, despite the fact that a number of children with these difficulties were being placed in mainstream schools at this time.

The inconsistencies of SEN provision within schools, along with the lack of a clear and coherent policy for pupils with SEN across the country, resulted in a build-up of pressure for change on the Government throughout the 1960s. On the one hand, there was a growing concern about pupils who were regarded as ineducable, to the extent that this led to the removal of this category in the Education Act of 1970. On the other hand, there was pressure from some parents and teachers of children in special schools for their integration into mainstream schools.

THE WARNOCK REPORT AND THE EDUCATION ACT (1981)

During the early 1970s the pressure for change was overwhelming, to the point that in 1972 the Government set up a committee of enquiry, chaired by Mary Warnock. Its remit was to report on the whole field of special education provision and its recommendations were to have a major influence on the subsequent direction of special educational policy in England and Wales.

Estimating the proportion of pupils in schools who had SEN was a major concern of the Warnock Committee. When it reported (DES 1978) the Warnock Committee confirmed earlier figures from Burt (1931), Schonell (1941) and the DES (1971), that up to one in five or up to 20 per cent of pupils were in need of SEN provision. Further, it argued that this was neither a static figure, which would remain constant throughout the years of compulsory schooling, nor an indication of the proportion of pupils to be found in every school.

This was a far larger percentage than that used in other developed countries. A figure of between 3 and 6 per cent of the school population with SEN is a common figure in most European countries (e.g. Italy: Roda 1991; Norway: Helgerland 1992; Belgium: Detraux and Dens 1992). The proportion of children identified in the United States is around 4 per cent (Booth 1982c).

The Warnock Report suggested that around that time some 2 per cent of pupils would have sufficient difficulties to warrant placement in special schools. These pupils, it recommended, should be identified and formally assessed through a statement of special educational need. This would carry with it a legally binding educational contract between the pupil and the LEA which was to be undertaken by the school and be subject to an annual review to monitor progress. The Committee indicated that it expected that resources would be made available to implement their recommendations.

Mary Warnock argued that the Report contained nothing new, rather its recommendations were based on existing good practice to be found in schools. The Report recommended that the statutory categories detailed in the 1944 Education Act should be discontinued and the concept of special education should be widened. Children so described should have their needs assessed systematically and regularly and these records should be maintained by schools. This assessment process should involve five stages. Each of these stages would see an increasing involvement of greater professional expertise.

The Warnock Report suggested that access to the record kept by schools, with the exception of sensitive material of a professional nature, should be available to parents. Parents would be encouraged to be involved during the assessment of their children. To help them they should have a 'named person' as a point of contact. The Report suggested that during the period of compulsory schooling this should be the child's head teacher.

Other recommendations in the Report called for an expansion of the advisory and support services provided by each LEA, training for more educational psychologists to be made available, better co-ordination between the various professional organisations involved, a major expansion of teacher education at both pre- and post-qualification stages to aid the development of classroom teachers in the are of SEN and the development of a group to promote and co-ordinate research in this area of education.

The Report was published without dissension, all of the members signing it without reservation. Mary Warnock regarded this as one of its greatest strengths. A further strength, noted by Adams (1986) was that criticisms of it were minimal and the reception which it received nationally was generally one of welcome and agreement. Richmond (1979) was even more strident, arguing that its reception was one of unqualified assent. Bushell (1979) described it as vital to the future of special education. This positive response was also reflected by Sayer (1981), Tansley and Pankhurst (1981) and Evans (1982). The NAS/UWT (1983, p. 1) went as far as to describe the effect of the Report as 'being to change the face of special education in this country'.

On a political level, criticisms were low key and focused mainly on its financial implications, rather than the philosophical stance that was taken. This stance was endorsed by the Government. There was widespread official support for the philosophical base of the Report, the general direction of its proposals and its main thrust.

As had happened so many times before with reports of commissions on special education, despite the positive reaction to the Warnock Report, publication coincided with major domestic economic and social problems. The 'winter of discontent' of 1979 was a cruel blow to those who were looking for considerable funding for the recommended changes. The consequence was a White Paper that made no promise of extra financial resources above those already budgeted to promote change. As a result of this the Bill that emerged mainly as a consequence of the report was received with muted criticism. One MP described it as 'Warnock without resources'. Neil Kinnock, in a parliamentary debate, regarded it as being akin to Brighton pier in relation to a trip to France; OK as far as it went, but not much use overall!

The 1981 Act embodied many of the recommendations of the

Warnock Report. The Act made it clear that not all children recommended for a statement of SEN would receive one. The DES Circular 1/83 outlined criteria for statementing in terms of *prima facie* grounds which would indicate that children's needs were such as to require provision additional to, or otherwise different from the facilities and resources generally available in ordinary schools in the area. The Act acknowledged the concept of special education detailed in the 1944 Act concerning those in 'need of special educational treatment'. However, the Warnock Report widened the age range to be accommodated to include children from two to 19 years.

Adams (1986) argued that within the Act there were two legal concepts of special education: learning difficulties and provision. The 1981 Act defined a learning difficulty in three ways. The first relates to children who have significantly greater difficulties in learning than the majority of children of their age. The second is concerned with children who have a disability which prevents or hinders them from making use of educational facilities of the kind provided in schools. The third relates to children who are under five years of age, and would have difficulties on entering school, if special educational provision were not made for them.

The concept of special educational provision was defined by Adams (1986) in terms of a child attaining the age of two who needs educational provision which is in addition to or otherwise different from that which is made generally available in the mainstream schools.

The emphasis of the Warnock Report was mainly on provision based on the level of ability of individual children and the pace at which they could work. Extra resources were to be provided through the formally organised statementing procedure.

The 1981 Education Act also formalised various important recommendations contained within the Warnock Report (1978). These included: the involvement of parents in the assessment procedure, the principle of a continuum of need rather than categories of handicap, provision for the assessment of children under the age of two years, the establishment of new and formalised links between the various professional agencies responsible for the care and welfare of children with SEN, and formalising the duties of the LEAs to ensure that the education of pupils with SEN would be undertaken in mainstream schools.

The 1981 Education Act acted more positively than any previous report to galvanise action throughout the country and to focus more sharply on provision for children with SEN. In this respect it can be regarded as having been partially successful. However, despite the indications in the report that not all children who were recommended for a statement of SEN would receive one, the floodgates of expectation were opened.

The impact of the 1981 Act varied across the country. It not only raised expectations for the greater inclusion of pupils with SEN into mainstream schools but also created tensions between parents teachers and local authorities with respect to the availability of resources to meet this. The Audit Commission/HMI Report (1992) identified three particular concerns. These were: clarifying the definition of SEN and the respective responsibilities of the LEAs and schools, a lack of accountability by both schools and LEAs for progress of pupils and of accountability of the schools as to the resources they received from the LEA for SEN and the lack of incentives which existed for LEAs to fully implement the 1981 Act.

THE EDUCATION ACT (1993)

As a result of the tensions created by the 1981 Act, educational provision for pupils with SEN has been further regularised in recent years through the impact of the 1993 Education Act and particularly the introduction of the Code of Practice. The Code of Practice on the identification and assessment of pupils with special educational needs (DfE 1994) was issued as guidance on the implementation of Section Three of the 1993 Education Act which was concerned with SEN provision. The legislation clarified and updated aspects of the 1981 Act.

A DfE consultation paper (1993) had set out proposals with regard to the rights of parents of children with special educational needs. It proposed that parents rights over the choice of school should be extended, the time taken by LEAs to make assessments and statements should be reduced and rights of appeal for parents should be extended. It also proposed that an independent tribunal should be established to replace the jurisdiction of both the Secretary of State and the LEA committees to hear appeals under the 1981 Act.

Blatch (1993) in a House of Lords debate, set the parameters for change around six principles. These related to the identification and assessment of special educational needs as quickly and easily as possible and the use of the most appropriate agencies for provision. She indicated that schools were to receive clear guidelines on how best to identify, assess and monitor children with special educational needs. Schools and LEAs were also to be given clear criteria as to when statutory assessments may be necessary. LEAs were also to receive guidance on the procedure they should adopt when making assessments and statements and in naming an appropriate school for children. She argued that guidance, along with the regulations and the Bill, promised a commonly understood and acceptable framework for provision for all children with SEN.

The Code is not a mandatory document, rather it is set out as guidelines for school development. Eric Forth (1994), then a junior minister at the Department of Education, expressed the view that it should be based on the fundamental principles of good practice which had been developed over the previous years. This was set out in the Code (paras 5 and 7, pp. i–ii) in terms of 'guidance designed to help schools make effective decisions and for which LEAs must have regard'.

The Code, in indicating that SEN provision is a matter for the school as a whole, also detailed the responsibilities of the major partners in the decisions that have to be made. This involves a five stage model for assessment and intervention, which includes a role for all who work with pupils with SEN. It states that the governors and the head teacher should reflect on the way their school identifies, assesses and makes provision for pupils with SEN and ensures that this information is publicly available.

The governing body has the responsibility to keep an oversight of the work within the school in this area, determine SEN policy and establish appropriate staffing and funding arrangements. Head teachers are responsible for the management strategies and liaison between themselves the governors and the SEN co-ordinator. The SEN co-ordinator is responsible for the daily operation of the policy and its co-ordination, particularly at stages 2 and 3. The rest of the teaching and non-teaching staff should also be involved in the development of policy and have a responsibility to express concerns about those pupils whom they consider might be at risk.

The non-prescriptive format of the Code of Practice extends to its overall framework. This is set out as a partnership between the school, the LEA, the parents and the child with SEN within a five-stage assessment and intervention process. It is true that the Audit Commission/HMI Report (1992) indicated this format had already been widely adopted in many LEAs, with varying degrees of effectiveness, and with some LEAs reducing the number of stages from five to three or four. In this respect the framework of the Code was based on the development of good practice within schools.

Hegarty (1995, p. 40) commented that the Code was 'a singularly important document for schools (which) should undoubtedly help them make better provision for pupils with special educational needs'. However, recent evidence from large scale surveys by

OFSTED (1996), the NUT (1996) and work by Garner (1995), Dyson and Gains (1995) Stakes (1996) and Kane (1996) have indicated that its introduction has not been met without difficulties. A wide variety of views have been expressed about the introduction of the Code of Practice (1994). These have ranged from considerable optimism (Harvey 1995) to undisguised pessimism (Webster 1994). Hornby (1995, p. 116), in a review of the literature, described overall opinions as 'ambivalent'.

The positive points that have emerged in the OFSTED (1996) report included: the amount of hard work that has been done by teachers in a short period of time to make the Code effective; the level of understanding of its demands by teachers and the widespread appointment of SENCOs in the schools. These last two points were also acknowledged in the NUT (Lewis *et al* 1995) survey. This survey indicated that over 99 per cent of schools had appointed a SENCO in their school.

The negative points of the OFSTED report included: inadequate resourcing and financial arrangements within schools; the extra workload included in the tasks such as the writing of Individual Education Programmes (IEPs) or the extra time needed for liaison work with colleagues and the development of assessment procedures in schools.

The NUT report (1995) is largely negative in tone. Their survey which included about 9 per cent of the nation's schools, indicated large-scale dissatisfaction at the introduction of the Code of Practice. It indicated that in primary schools over 50 per cent of SENCOs were also classroom teachers with other responsibilities and one third were head teachers.

The burden of work for some 50 per cent of SENCOs in primary schools and 25 per cent of secondary schools was generally not alleviated by specific non-contact time. The OFSTED report (1996) found that the amount of time allocated to the work involved varied widely from school to school, with some schools committing very little time to the required tasks. The NUT and OFSTED surveys were supported by Dyson and Gains (1995) and Stakes (1996) in identifying complaints from SENCOs. These were related to the bureaucratic nature of the Code of Practice and the excess of paperwork which it generated.

It is arguable that the number of pupils with IEPs has multiplied enormously in the past two years. This has been compounded by the need to place children with behavioural difficulties on the SEN register creating a new category of SEN. The increase in the number of pupils so categorised has increased the workload of teachers and created many difficulties for SENCOs. One contributory factor is the large number of pupils being categorised as having SEN. As indicated earlier, the 20 per cent of pupils considered to have SEN in the UK is a far greater proportion of the school population identified by our European partners.

The number of pupils with SEN has had an effect on resourcing. Hornby (1995) when discussing this in relation to the successful implementation of the Code of Practice (1994) argued that the allocation of no extra financial resources could be seen as part of a deliberate strategy by the Government to reduce the overall cost of SEN provision. In line with this suggestion, certain LEAs have introduced changes in their assessment procedures to lower the threshold levels of pupil achievement for them to receive extra help or to be considered for a statement of special educational need. By reducing the number of pupils in this way costs have also been reduced.

The OFSTED report also indicated that there was a vagueness, particularly in some primary schools, about how the money for SEN provision was being spent. They reported that in some schools SENCOs had little idea of the basis for SEN funding. Further points that emerged from their enquiry were concerns over: the need to support the work of SENCOs in schools; the need for greater governor and parental knowledge about the working of the Code of Practice (1994), better inter-school liaison to facilitate the exchange of information on pupils with SEN and the need to add all pupils with behavioural difficulties to the school SEN register.

Garner (1995) identified areas of concern relating to the policy aspects of the Code as well as its roles and procedures. The issues identified included: raising staff awareness; the management of time the development of a whole-school policy; working with other agencies and monitoring and reviewing children's progress. These were clearly identifiable as major features that were broadly consistent across those teachers who were surveyed. There is also a growing feeling that the Code demands an unrealistic level of expertise in SEN among classroom teachers and co-ordinators. Some staffs are left with a feeling of being overwhelmed by the range of expertise they are expected to have and the depth of information they are expected to hold.

School SEN co-ordinators have also had to build up school resources and in some cases become involved in the testing of children in a much more formal way than previously. Further, there continue to be problems over overall resourcing. Blatch (Hansard 1993) indicated that the operation of the Code was to be placed within 'a finite sum of money' and that there was 'no blank cheque operating anywhere in the public services'. This continues to be particularly difficult in a situation where the accepted tradition of SEN resourcing has been by demand and when both parental and professional expectations are set.

A survey undertaken by the National Confederation of Parent–Teachers' Associations (1996) in 1 100 schools indicated that some 60 per cent of schools were having difficulties in meeting the Code's demands within their budgetary limits.

Similarly, Kane (1996) has been very critical. He has argued that although most teachers are in favour of its broad aims there are major difficulties in its implementation. His view is that implementation at classroom level is compounded by discrepancies in both national and local policy and planning. Thus, in different areas of the country there are different levels of resources and different priorities to the extent that, in his view, many children will go through their schooling without any positive measures being taken to address their special needs. In his view, the whole concept of the integration of pupils with SEN in mainstream schools must be questioned. He argued that this is particularly the case in relation to the needs of other pupils in the mainstream school. Further, the complex behavioural difficulties exhibited by many pupils with SEN has not only increased stress on teachers but has also had a negative effect on the quality of learning for other pupils.

CONCLUSIONS

The legislation which has been introduced to facilitate changes in the development of educational provision for pupils with SEN has, throughout the period of compulsory schooling, been largely dependent on the pressures exerted by interested individuals and pressure groups working on behalf of children with SEN. There is little indication of a strong political will to initiate and implement constructive change. Where governments have set up committees these have been as a result of considerable pressure from parent and teacher groups. The recommendations which have been made by these committees have subsequently often been watered down or ignored.

Development has also been inhibited by the nature of the legislation, which has resulted in recommendations, guidelines and advice to LEAs and schools rather than in a mandatory framework. The thrust of this legislation has been dissipated to some extent by the structure of government in the UK which relies on the willingness of individual LEAs to interpret and implement the legislation positively.

More recently, there has been a greater direction of policy from the centre. Examples of this include the Code of Practice (1994) backed up by OFSTED inspections. However, it is clear that this approach has produced organisational difficulties which need to be addressed. These difficulties are compounded by the percentage of children considered to be in need of SEN provision in the UK. This is considerably greater than in other democracies in the Western world. As a result of this there are implications for both the management and dissemination of available resources. These issues will be discussed in some detail in subsequent chapters.

— 3

Provision and resources for SEN

INTRODUCTION

Difficulties in improving provision for pupils with SEN in mainstream schools have occurred, partly, as a consequence of inadequate resources. The consistent lack of appropriate resourcing can be closely linked to the overall lack of political commitment noted in the previous chapter and to the general attitude to pupils with SEN in the wider society which is discussed in the next chapter. The resources referred to include teaching and support personnel as well as textbooks and specialist equipment for pupils with SEN. Staffing SEN provision is expensive because of its labour intensive nature. Textbooks are similarly expensive, as is the purchasing of specialist equipment. Difficulties in this area are compounded at times of economic difficulty. In the education service special education has often been among the first areas to experience financial cuts.

This chapter will consider the development of resources for pupils with SEN in mainstream schools and discuss how the level of resourcing has affected changes in provision for them. It will take account of the deployment of both human and material resources to aid changes in provision. Particular attention will be paid to the development of material resources to aid the assessment and learning development of pupils with SEN. Attention will also be paid to criticisms of the lack of resources for SEN provision which can be identified from both official and unofficial reports and the effect which this has on overall provision for such pupils in mainstream schools.

ASSESSMENT

The development of resources for assessing the level of achievement and the potential of pupils was one of the most important areas of progress for children with SEN in the early part of the century. Originally, formal assessments were provided by psychologists in order to identify and assess the needs of children with SEN. More recent developments have made tests more accessible to classroom teachers. The importance of this development, in terms of its effect on the development of SEN provision throughout the century, cannot be underestimated. Ferneaux (1969) attributed the importance of the work of pioneers such as Binet and Burt to laying the base for much subsequent practice in the field of special education.

Research on human intelligence testing began with the work of Binet in France during the early years of the twentieth century. In Britain, among the first to see the value of this development were Burt (who adapted Binet's work to suit English conditions) Spearman, Thompson, Duncan and Schonell.

During the inter-war period there were considerable advances in the practice of testing and it became much more widespread during this period. Knowledge gained from the formal testing process helped to provide better information on pupils with SEN and helped to change the approach to them. In Britain much of the responsibility for this change derived from the work of Burt and his influence on the study of child psychology. Burt (1921, 1935, 1937) considered that some 15 per cent of pupils in school could be regarded as having learning difficulties which could create problems in mainstream schools. Schonell (1942) confirmed Burt's figures, indicating that some 17 per cent of pupils were in this category. Both of these surveys indicated a higher percentage of pupils than the Wood Report (1929), which proposed that 10 per cent of pupils had SEN.

Burt (1921) also argued for the categorisation of pupils with SEN into three distinct groups. These were similar to those described in the Wood Report (1929) and detailed in the 1921 Education Act. However, Burt argued such categories should be flexible, certainly more so than indicated by some of the members of the Wood Committee. Burt (1921) went to great lengths to point out that any categorisation could not be seen as an infallible guide or as able to provide definitive cut off points.

Burt's most important contribution during the inter-war period was his work with pupils who were by his definition dull and who were most commonly found in mainstream schools. He detailed two distinct categories of dull pupils: those whose backwardness was accidental or acquired and those for whom it was 'innate or permanent' (1937, p. 605). This definition also distinguished between those pupils who may be regarded as exhibiting long-term difficulties which may persist throughout their entire school career and beyond and those who may, for whatever reason, have specific difficulties which could be remedied in the short term. This distinction was also used by Schonell (1942). Its importance can be gauged by its influence throughout much of the century. It was a description which Tansley and Gulliford (1960) the DES (1969, 1979) and the Warnock Report (1978) subscribed to many years later.

Approaches to the assessment of pupils with SEN have been a victim of educational fashion. For example, the use of intelligence quotients (IQs) as indicators of children's potential were for many years a key aspect of the selection procedure for grammar school as part of the eleven plus examination. From the 1950s onwards there has been a growing concern about the cultural bias inherent in IQ tests and the lack of stability in IQ scores. Confidence in their ability to determine children's potential at the age of 11 was gradually eroded and contributed to the abandonment of the eleven plus selection exam.

In the second half of the century the role of formal assessments became gradually more and more unfashionable until the advent of the National Curriculum (1988) and the Code of Practice (1994) brought about a change. The overall emphasis on testing described in the National Curriculum documentation along with the development of individual education programmes (IEPs) and the greater emphasis on a discrepancy model for identifying specific learning difficulties required by the Code of Practice has led to a resurgence in their influence.

'MEDICAL' MODEL OF ASSESSMENT

The influence of the medical profession has continued throughout the whole period. Their influence is clearly seen in the Code of Practice (1994). It is evident not only in the work of the pioneer educational psychologists and the development of the school's psychological service but also through the key role which doctors have played in assessing pupils for special schools. The approach taken by many practising teachers also showed the influence of the medical model. The use of words such as diagnosis, the application of remedies for pupils and the formal assessment of work and the pupil's abilities to inform remediation indicated an approach very similar to that of the local doctor working with patients.

The value of this approach with pupils with SEN has been a source of considerable debate, with particularly strong criticisms of it being raised in the immediate pre-Warnock era. Criticisms were raised particularly in relation to assessment procedures. Buddenhagen (1967) claimed that the concept of IQ is only a triviality. Tizard

(1973) concurred, arguing that current assessment procedures were time consuming, lacked relevance and were of little use. Further criticisms were also raised by Clarke and Clarke (1975), who argued that assessments which were made outside the classroom situation, in artificially constructed circumstances, were so unrealistic as to provide information which was of little use.

The influence of the IQ test in assessment procedures was similarly criticised. Buddenhagen (1967) argued that IQ scores should be seen as a capacity for growth within a person, rather than a fixed assessment of mental capacity. Clarke (1967) was even more scathing, describing the IQ test as being discredited when used as the only form of assessment. Jones (1975) although not dismissing the use of such tests altogether, strongly supported the views of Cohen and Mannion (1992) and Cave and Maddison (1978). They argued that assessment was only part of the procedure and that the goal of all assessment was help for the child.

CLASSROOM RESOURCES

The question of the suitability of the curriculum for all pupils in the mainstream school had already been raised by the early twentieth century. The views expressed by Burt (1937) and Schonell (1942) with regard to the categorisation of pupils with learning difficulties enhanced this. It was becoming increasingly clearer that pupils with short term learning problems would need a different form of curricular provision from those with long term difficulties. Furthermore, these differences needed to be accommodated and resourced in the mainstream school, with all the consequent implications for the management and organisational skills of the classroom teacher.

Developments in this area were somewhat slow in coming. Sampson (1975) indicated that it was not until the 1930s that differences had begun to emerge in the provision made by teachers for the two categories described by Burt as 'dull'. Sampson indicated that such developments continued to be haphazard and inconsistent, with many children with SEN coping as best they could in mainstream classes.

Developments in classroom practice coincided with the development of a more 'child-centred' culture towards pupils with learning difficulties in mainstream schools. This approach, which was more concerned with the personal needs and individual development of pupils rather than allowing them to flounder on the traditional curriculum, was accompanied by the growth of learning resources to support it. However, this cannot be regarded as a widespread trend.

Rather, it was limited to the work of individual teachers. Examples of this approach were discussed by Baron (1938), Hill (1939) and Duncan (1942). Duncan in particular advocated an approach that was described as involving practical activities based on the five senses rather than 'verbalisation' and 'theory'. Sampson (1975) produced evidence of such approaches in the period before the beginning of the Second World War in 1939. This indicated that much of the motivation for this work rested on the interest and experimentation of individual teachers.

READING CENTRES

The introduction of formal assessment procedures had a number of practical implications in the development of new resources. In the immediate post-war period one such initiative was the development of centres for pupils with reading difficulties, which some local authorities set up outside the provision of mainstream schools.

In practical terms these centres were set up as a result of an apparent decline in standards of reading which occurred as a result of the disruption to schooling caused by the Second World War. General concern was shown nationally about this and evidence collected by HMIs indicated the seriousness of the situation. It was hoped that such developments would bring about changes in the way reading was taught.

The philosophy behind reading centres came from the views of Burt (1937). He advocated that such developments were essential in the interests of all parties: the pupils, their teachers and other children in the school. He argued that the best approach for such developments would be through the formation of separate classes, either as part of the school or organised externally to it. This, in his view, would allow pupils to be taught at a more appropriate pace to suit their needs and for them to be given appropriate diagnosis and treatment.

Accounts of such centres were given by Birch (1948) and Schonell and Wall (1949). These centres were set up specifically for that group of pupils described by Schonell as 'backward' or 'retarded'. In reality the situation was highly selective in certain respects. Schonell and Wall (1949)indicated that each child selected had an IQ of at least 90 and maladjusted children (*sic*) were excluded so that the groups would not be disrupted.

Essentially each group was small (some five to eight pupils). Each child was selected on the basis of diagnostic and psychological testing, and both the child and its parents were involved in the work of

the centre. It was seen as crucial that when undertaking the programme of study no child should be allowed to fail. Birch (1948)
described his centre as systematic and purposeful, while Schonell
and Wall (1949) wrote similarly of a systematic and planned
approach to children's difficulties. The atmosphere within the centres was deliberately positive and the freedom to experiment was
encouraged.

Results in terms of the progress in reading skills of those children
who attended were encouraging. Birch (1948) reported they were
higher than expected, while Schonell and Wall (1949) concluded that
the children responded fairly rapidly to the teaching provided.

The news of the positive results from these clinics spread to other
local authorities and there was a proliferation of similar centres in
various parts of the country. Sampson (1975) claimed that the work
of those such as Birch (1948) and Schonell and Wall (1949) was so
influential that it spurred on somewhat similar developments in secondary schools throughout the country. Further, she argued that
much that was characteristic of 'remedial education' at that time
could be traced to these initiatives.

Despite the fact that the early reading clinics were generally considered to have had some success, criticisms of them were raised.
Collins (1972), Topping (1975) and Sewell (1981) argued that
research conducted on children who attended the clinics indicated
that the reading levels achieved at the time of leaving them was not
sustained after the extra help was withdrawn and the pupils returned
to their normal classes in the mainstream school. Rutter *et al* (1970)
indicated that the special classes they observed in a survey they had
conducted had not been successful in meeting the needs of children
with specific reading retardation, the very aim of the classes at their
inception.

Collins (1972) also argued that the approach of the reading centres
had little scientific basis, while Edwards (1983) criticised them for
their essentially pseudo medical model approach. May-Wilson and
Broadhead (1979) also pointed out that the approach used by pioneers such as Schonell and Wall was so technical and far removed
from teachers working in schools that many mainstream school
teachers were not able to translate the findings into good classroom
practice. They argued that such a mystique had been built up around
the approaches used in the clinics that it was in danger of becoming
removed from the practice of the classroom teacher. Hughes (1982)
and Hanko (1985) wrote similarly, pointing out that those specialist
teachers in this field were not only working in isolation from their
mainstream colleagues but also widening the gap between them.

Despite these criticisms, the development of reading clinics acted as a spur to a growing commitment to work on reading development of children with SEN. Similarly, these developments encouraged the work of educational psychologists. They have been traced by Sintra (1981), Bowman (1981) and Swann (1982) as part of the work of the Schools' Psychological Service. This was an area of growing influence throughout the 1950s. Swann (1982) described it as leading to the establishment of a 'power base', which has remained ever since.

A WIDENING OF PROVISION

The development of provision for pupils with SEN at school level continued throughout the 1950s. The evidence indicates that this was patchy. Change was largely dependent on the work of individuals. Some LEAs and individual schools developed provision, while in others very little seemed to be done.

An enquiry by Collins (1972) provided a useful insight into contemporary provision in the secondary school. His report showed that the situation was that there were a considerable variety of names to describe the work that was being undertaken in school, including progress, adjustment, opportunity and improvement classes. In general, these classes were usually small with about twenty pupils in each and concentrated almost exclusively on the teaching of reading and basic English skills. He found that two forms of organisation were commonly used to support this work: groups of pupils within an individual school or, as in reading clinics, groups brought together from a variety of adjacent schools.

Children with learning difficulties, particularly in secondary schools, were often placed in the same class. Those with long-term problems remained there for most of their secondary school life. For some, described by Chapman (1959), Hargreaves (1967), Holt (1964), Partridge (1966) and Willis (1977) this approach only accentuated their problems and confirmed their lack of ability to both their peers and teachers.

Chapman (1969) described provision for SEN in secondary modern schools. These schools which were set up as part of the tripartite system of secondary education after the 1944 Act were designated for those pupils who were regarded to be of a more practical nature. In reality, these schools were regarded as the lowest tier of the system: after the grammar school (for the most academically able) and the technical school (for children with technical skills), secondary modern schools provided for about half the age group.

In the 1950s secondary schools made little specific provision for their pupils with SEN. From one point of view the architecture of the new secondary schools did not help the formation of small groups of pupils. The vast majority of the classrooms were built to a standard size for a class of about 30 pupils and specialist accommodation was virtually non-existent.

The lack of specific help for pupils with SEN was reflected in the work of Chapman (1969) who reported that provision for such pupils in the secondary modern school was not considered as a separate issue, but as part of the subject-based approach. In the post-Warnock era this might be regarded as a sound approach to the development of good practice with the needs of children being met within each subject area and the curriculum content matched to children's abilities. However, in reality this was largely an indication of a lack of overall provision for those with SEN. Chapman (1969) provided no indication of any teacher being made responsible for working with pupils with SEN in schools. This is confirmed by Cleugh (1961), the Cheshire Education Committee (1963) and Gulliford (1969) as well as both the findings and the recommendations made in the Newsom Report (1963).

Where mention is made in the literature of the late 1950s and the early 1960s to some form of provision for the less able in the mainstream school, the indications are that this was undertaken with pupils in their first two years after transfer (years 7 and 8). There is little indication of any provision being made after this, or of what percentage of pupils were successfully moved back to mainstream classes.

The subject-based approach described by Chapman (1969) is significant in that this was how the resources of the majority of secondary schools were organised. The literature indicates a limited deployment of resources for those with SEN in schools. This supports the view that little work was done with pupils over the age of 13 who continued to have reading difficulties. The general pattern of organisation was class based work with one teacher, often a general subject teacher without special educational training, who would be timetabled with this group of pupils for between 50 and 75 per cent of their timetable. The Cheshire Education Committee Report (1963) argued for a change in approach. The Committee claimed that a better approach would be for responsible staff, with the experience of this type of work, to be used to organise and co-ordinate the work relating to these pupils throughout the school. Gulliford (1969) supported this view, pointing out the need for better training of teachers to meet the needs of such pupils more effectively and at the same time called for a specialist to organise provision.

THE NEWSOM REPORT

The Newsom Report, 'Half our Future' (1963) was an important influence on change in the mid-1960s. The Report called for classes specifically for pupils with SEN to be kept to a minimum. This was from both the pupils' and the teachers' point of view. This, it was argued, would allow those with SEN to maintain social contact with other pupils in the school. The report called for a form of examination for secondary modern school pupils to be taken at sixteen. It was from this that the Certificate of Secondary Education (CSE) evolved. In reality, although this exam was very influential in both modern and comprehensive schools, it was not aimed at all the school population, and those pupils with learning difficulties (the 18 per cent described by Warnock) were generally not expected to take many CSEs.

Although it was a major influence on thinking and practice in schools throughout the mid-1960s, the Newsom Report provided little indication of the direction which SEN provision should take. It could be argued that this was not the main remit of the report. However, bearing in mind that the Warnock Report (1978) indicated that up to 20 per cent of the population as a whole had special educational needs and there would be a heavier concentration of them within secondary modern schools, it is clear that the report concentrated far too little on this section of the school population.

What was becoming clearer at the time of the Newsom Report was the diversity of approaches being used in schools where SEN provision had been made. Sampson and Pumfrey (1970) identified seven models of provision for special education. These they described as: class-based teaching, withdrawal groups, withdrawal for individual help, a combination of class-based teaching and group withdrawal, a combination of class-based teaching and individual help and a combination of all three approaches.

The DES (1971) also noted a wide variety of approaches. This survey also noted a considerable diversity of views on the best way of organising SEN provision. This situation was partly accounted for by the variety of possible organisational strategies which were available. It was clear that some co-ordination was needed. The wide variety of approaches reflected more the views of teachers than the needs of pupils. Attempts were made to outline the best of these and to look for ways forward. Westwood (1975) outlined various ways in which provision could be developed. In his approach the accent was on the development of good classroom practice. Sampson and Pumfrey (1970) made similar points, particularly in relation to the staffing of such approaches. They were particularly concerned to draw experience and expertise from a combination of full-time and part-time staff.

PROVISION IN SCHOOLS

Despite the difficulties over provision for SEN the DES (1964) expressed optimism in the overall situation as it had been observed by school inspectors. It was argued that much progress had been made since the 1944 Act and that what had been achieved could be seen with some justifiable pride. Their reasoning was related to the overall provision of better schools and facilities, greater knowledge of the emotional and intellectual characteristics of pupils, wider interest and sympathy for them, and good careers guidance.

The DES (1964) also indicated that a good deal needed to be done, particularly in relation to curriculum provision, which it indicated was less successfully adapted in the mainstream school than that found in the special school. Criticisms were also raised in this report over the direction and style of the curriculum programme in mainstream schools. The over-specialisation of subject teaching in the modern schools was, it argued, inimical to the best interests of many children, confining those with learning difficulties in particular to unrelated fields of learning in which pupils found it almost impossible to see any coherent pattern. The document called for one teacher to be responsible for much of the work of their class throughout the week.

By 1971 however, the DES (1971) were stating that the picture painted some seven years earlier had changed markedly and they were now indicating that all was far from well. It was suggested that in a period of rapid change in secondary schools it was hardly surprising that in some schools, confronted with many difficulties, the needs of the slowest pupils seemed to have been given less than a fair share of consideration.

Comments from other quarters were more direct. Smedley, in a speech to the National Conference on backward children in 1963, described the general attitude to the organisation of provision for pupils with SEN in secondary schools as ambivalent, with only a partial commitment from society towards the provision of resources. Bell (1970) described the resources available as inadequate, commenting further that overall planning for pupils with SEN was virtually non-existent. He argued that there were a number of areas where this could be observed. These included: a lack of continuity between the primary and secondary phases of schooling, too much dependence on the interests of the head teacher, the major burden resting on individual teachers and the continuing shortage of well-trained teachers for pupils in need of extra help.

These points were also made by Jackson (1966) who argued for the importance of school based help from specialist staff or their colleagues to advise them about such children. Banks and Findlayson (1973) emphasised the importance of good timetabling for these pupils and argued that the standard of timetabling in the secondary modern school in particular needed to be raised to meet their needs. They argued that particular attention needed to be given to the low concentration span and short-term memory of some pupils, as well as the more practical nature of their abilities.

Westwood (1975) was scathing with regard to SEN provision in the secondary school, describing it as a graveyard of human potential. He regarded the overall situation as tantamount to a national scandal. Brennan (1971) was equally vitriolic in his assessment, claiming that those children with SEN who did not enter special schools were left in the most hazardous situation in the education system. He asserted that their educational future was at the mercy of completely fortuitous circumstances, which differed not only from area to area but also from school to school or even from term to term within the same school. Sampson and Pumfrey (1970) described the situation similarly. It was their view that current practice was based on opinion and convenience rather than research evidence.

It would seem that the apparent complacency of the 1964 DES report was misplaced and provision for the less able in secondary schools was no different from that of the rest of the school population which had been described by Birley (1972, p. 1) as 'diffused', 'vague' and 'haphazard' and by Midwinter (1972) as a mishmash of the product of laws, individual ideas, the architectural design of schools, social change and acts of God.

RESOURCING AND THE WARNOCK REPORT

The central remit of the Warnock Committee (1978) was to provide recommendations to aid the development of provision for pupils with SEN in schools. They held the view that all schools had the responsibility to identify and help pupils with such needs. Further, all mainstream schools should, where it was practicable, be encouraged to accommodate pupils with SEN alongside their peers. For this to occur there was a need for continued organisational and curriculum development as well as adequate resourcing.

Bines (1989) has argued that the organisation of the individual school is a key factor in the development of any policy for children with SEN. In her view the relationship between the staff working directly with such children and the rest of the staff is crucial. Hegarty (1986) also argued that changes in working practices for all staff in the school were essential and considered that such an approach would benefit all who worked there.

The practical difficulties in developing such provision cannot be underestimated. Daniels (1982) described such developments as problematical, while Clunies-Ross *et al* (1982) saw them as a considerable challenge. Hegarty and Pocklington (1982) were clear that mainstream schools operated under certain constraints and that success for pupils with SEN could be measured, at least in part, in terms of circumventing these, and capitalising on the opportunities presented.

In the years after the 1981 Act mainstream schools came under increased scrutiny in every aspect of their work. The SEN department was no exception. HMI (1990) were particularly critical of provision. They indicated that children with statements were not benefiting optimally from the provision which was being made for them. Their criticisms embraced such issues as curricula, the modification of teaching approaches to accommodate the needs of individuals and the proper resourcing of departments. Further criticisms included the provision of suitable accommodation for pupils and the training of staff to meet the needs of the pupils. Weddell (1988) suggested that although the 1981 Act had set the tone for change there continued to be wide variations in the provision that was available. One of the key factors in these variations was the role designated for the SEN department in schools. Another is as the consequence of the development of the policy of the local management of schools.

THE ROLE OF THE SEN DEPARTMENT

The importance of developments in the management of SEN provision in mainstream schools in the post-Warnock era cannot be underestimated. The role of SENCOs had to be determined as had the changing role of other specialist teachers. As part of an investigation into the role of SEN departments Dyson (1990, 1991, 1992) and Gains and Dyson (1993) undertook wide-ranging reviews. Their evidence indicated that many departments had run into overwhelming problems. The research indicated that the enthusiasm and commitment that was so evident in earlier years appeared destined to fail. Dyson (1991) argued that this was the case for two reasons. Firstly, SEN departmental staff faced major problems in attempting to bring other colleagues around to their way of thinking regarding their approach. This he saw as an unlikely prospect. Secondly, in relation to the advent of the National Curriculum and the effects of individualised curricula for every child, he argued that special education could no longer be defined in terms of the curriculum but in the approach to teaching it.

As a consequence it was argued that the co-ordinator in each school must actively seek out new roles. These, it was suggested by Gains and Dyson (1993) might be: the development of effective teaching strategies for all staff, teaching effective learning strategies to pupils with special educational needs and an increasingly more consultative role for SENCOs.

Changes in the pattern of working for specialist teachers were also identified. Both Gibbs (1987) and Evans and Lunt (1993) indicated changes in staff deployment. This they found was particularly so in the case of support service staff who were as likely to be undertaking advisory work with colleagues as working with individual pupils. They also found that teachers continued to want individual support for particular pupils as well as advice from other professionals. This has led to a large increase in the number of teachers and classroom assistants being assigned to this work over the last few years. The growth in this area has led to internal management problems in schools. These can be related to three major issues: the qualifications and experience of those employed in this way, their deployment on a day-to-day basis and the co-ordination of provision between schools and support services. A consequence of this has been growth in both the necessary liaison and the strategical management of SEN provision in schools.

THE LOCAL MANAGEMENT OF SCHOOLS

The introduction of local management of schools (LMS) allowed individual schools considerably greater control over the management of their own financial affairs. In its turn this has been a source of considerable change in the financing of provision for pupils with SEN in mainstream schools. The funding for pupils with SEN was a key question following the 1988 Act. Moore (1991) pointed out that the administrative requirements facing LEAs were enormous. Thus, at that time, he was uncertain whether the changes would favour pupils with SEN. He expressed his hope that through features such as quality assurance and service agreements between schools and other professional agencies it would ensure that what did evolve would be a significant improvement on current practice. The concept of buying-in services from other agencies such as educational psychologists or the LEA support service was new, and was one which was likely to have far reaching consequences.

This was also the case with opting out. Marshall, a DES staff inspector for SEN, told a Parents in Partnership conference (1987) of some of the difficulties. He emphasised particularly the reluctance of those schools that had opted out to cater for pupils with real and long-lasting difficulties. Leslie Marks at the same conference, warned that the new legislation, rather than enhancing the rights of such pupils, could be a backward step regarding their greater integration.

Surveys have indicated that a number of difficulties have occurred in this area. Lee (1992) suggested that some schools were confused over whether they should be targeting special needs on social or educational factors. He argued that this was creating a dilemma. Weddell (1988), Dessant (1989) and Russell (1990) expressed the view that contemporary educational philosophy was unhelpful to many pupils in the school system. They argued that, in an atmosphere where schools are pressured to produce good academic result and compete on such terms with others in their neighbourhood, it is likely that they have become less willing to accept and work with those pupils who are not going to enhance their reputation or status in the community. Mittler (1992) described this as the biggest threat to pupils with SEN in the ordinary school.

Further, evidence from newspaper reports during 1992 claimed that some LEAs were making provision for their pupils on financial rather than educational criteria and that the statementing procedure was no longer demand-led. A report by the Spastics Society (1992) supported this, stating that the greatest problem was a lack of money for the necessary provision. One LEA Educational Psychologist who contributed to this report indicated that certain LEAs were seeking ways of supporting children in schools in order to offset the need for expensive specialist placements.

Warnock (1993) also emphasised this point, commenting that LEAs continued to make educational decisions based on the resources at their disposal rather than on the needs of the individual child. She also indicated that the 1993 Education Act had compounded this problem even further and that the successful integration of pupils with SEN into mainstream schools was being slowed as a consequence.

Further, in the same newspaper article, she described her own 'naiveté to the point of idiocy' in not realising that national financial circumstances would mean that the only way for parents and schools to get appropriate arrangements was by statementing pupils. This has led, she has argued, to a situation where the largest percentage of children with SEN (the 18 per cent) are receiving inadequate resources to meet their needs. She claimed some children were 'slipping through the net'. This was a situation that was leaving them frustrated by their experiences of school and leading them towards truancy or exclusion.

The statementing process is a lengthy and frustrating process for some parents. This sadly contradicted the focus set in the Warnock Report (1978) which envisaged it as a helpful tool in the life of such pupils. The length of time that statements were taking to write (up to two years in some cases) and the lack of appropriate strategies and educational guidance for staff working with such pupils was causing concern, frustration and a general devaluation of the process. The Education Act (1993) stated that the process must be speeded up and set a target of six months for the whole process to be undertaken.

THE PRESENT SITUATION

The years between the Education Act of 1981 and that of 1988 were critical in the development of good practice in mainstream schools for children with SEN. This was particularly the case between the implementation of the 1981 Act in 1983 and 1988 when changes occurred in many schools. However, changes were often largely in philosophical approaches. The constructive features of the Warnock Report, along with the commitment of teachers responsible for children with SEN, helped to encourage a similar approach from many of their colleagues. This certainly had an effect on attitudes towards these children. However, in real terms many proposed changes were harder to implement and an element of 'lip service' emerged with staff in schools remaining largely unconvinced and sceptical about the practicalities of proposed changes. Where changes did occur these can be related to three aspects of provision. These were: the organisational and administrative changes which took place, changes to the curricular programme offered to such pupils and career development opportunities for staff working with them

A survey conducted by Hegarty (1982) showed that 97 per cent of staff felt there was a need for changes in both attitude and practice for pupils with SEN in mainstream schools. A similar group questioned by Lowdon (1984) indicated that more than 80 per cent of teachers felt this to be desirable, although it is important to point out that some 60 per cent of the returns showed some doubts about the practicalities of what was expected. Goacher *et al* (1986) provided similarly strong support for the philosophical approach of the Warnock Committee. This was particularly the case in relation to the replacement of the categories of handicap with the universal concept of special educational needs.

A review of the documentation emanating from LEAs at this time indicated that considerable variations of approach were being used up and down the country with consequent inconsistencies as far as provision and the fate of individual children were concerned. The situation in individual schools was similarly lacking in uniformity. Fish (1985, 1986), Butt (1989) and Stakes (1990) argued that the changes which were occurring were largely the result of efforts in individual schools. Hegarty (1987) described the situation as mixed and the continued patchiness as an indication that the overall pattern of provision had changed very little during this period. Both Hegarty and Pocklington (1982) and May-Wilson and Broadhead (1979) indicated that one of the problems was that pushing through any changes was dependent on the resources available. Further, there was the problem that many schools were neither properly equipped nor staffed to expand the work they were doing.

The overall philosophy of the ruling political party of the time (detailed in a White Paper 1985) with its emphasis on personal achievement, the survival of the fittest and with its focus on value for money, did not provide the best atmosphere to engage in a strong commitment to SEN. Again SEN was becoming an area of cost-cutting. A report by Lunt and Evans (1990) and another by the NUT (1993) indicated that in some LEAs discretionary services, such as support teaching teams for mainstream schools, were being cut as part of their necessary budget cuts. The NUT (1993) indicated that in the financial year 1991-92 some 10 per cent of LEAs had made cuts to special educational services. This was a situation that they argued was affecting individual schools' ability to provide for those with SEN.

The Report produced jointly by HMI and the Audit Commission (1992) showed wide variations in the quality of provision that was available for pupils with special needs in the mainstream school. Some LEAs were reported as showing a higher level of commitment and practice than others. The report indicated a general lack of clarification on the responsibilities of the officers, a lack of account-ability by the schools, some infighting between special school head teachers and their mainstream counterparts and a poor quality of monitoring of progress by some LEAs Further criticisms were made over the length of time that the statementing process took.

Curricular provision was similarly varied. HMI (1992) reported that some 28 per cent of lessons in mainstream schools were good or very good while in some 15 per cent children with SEN were not receiving a broad and balanced programme to meet the statutory requirements.

MATERIAL RESOURCES

Material resources for classroom use include the development and production of appropriate learning materials for pupils with SEN. These materials might include readers, subject texts and computer programmes as well as assessment materials. This is one area of provision where a steady improvement has been recorded which has helped both in the motivation and teaching of children with SEN, particularly those with learning difficulties.

Pupils with learning difficulties often had considerable problems with the standard texts that were available for the development of others in their peer group. For many years after the introduction of compulsory education there was little published material available and teachers had to produce their own to help some children. Although this was a feature across the whole curriculum, it was particularly the case with the development of reading skills.

Teachers often had to rely on material that was neither age nor interest appropriate for older pupils who had difficulties with reading. Material which was produced relied largely on the teacher's skills in matching their level of ability with appropriate material that was of interest to them.

In the period of expansion of provision in the 1970s (particularly during the period of the raising of the school leaving age in 1973 and the initiation of the adult literacy schemes around the same time) more suitable published material became available for use in schools. Greater consideration was given to both the reading age of the material and its interest age, as well as trying to make it more attractive for reluctant readers. This was particularly important for older pupils who had previously regarded much of what they had been presented with as childish and demotivating.

The trends that were set then have continued with an ever widening range of material available for teachers to use. There is a vast range of material available for children with SEN. The difficulties now are related much more to its selection bearing in mind the amount of money available. Careful selections now have to be made on the basis of the annual capitation allowance in the school set aside for SEN. In some schools, money is made available for this on an annual basis but the amount directed towards SEN is inconsistent, despite guidance from the DfEE relating to the money attached to children with SEN who are statemented. The SEN allocation continues to be largely dependent on internal school budgeting policy.

The introduction of computer software into the school curriculum since the mid-1980s has a marked effect on the learning strategies and opportunities for many pupils, not just those with SEN. This has been particularly the case with respect to their motivation. For pupils with SEN, developments in both computer hardware and software have been particularly useful. The range of activities available to aid their personal motivation and their learning development has increased considerably over the same period.

Software for children with SEN has developed from the simple skill-focused and merely mechanical approach to a much greater level of sophistication. Further, some of the packages that are available can be used with children of a wide range of ability, allowing pupils with SEN to participate fully in the activities. Particularly important in this area have been the development of word processing packages with grammar and spelling checks along with the use of colour copying facilities. Such packages have allowed children with SEN the opportunity to produce high quality work that would have been impossible through more conventional methods and allowed them to take a greater pride in the work that they have completed.

Resources available to assess pupils with SEN have also improved. The formal assessment procedures devised by Binet and adopted initially in the UK by Burt, which were discussed earlier in this chapter, were somewhat simplistic. Improvements over years have led to the development of much more sophisticated instruments. A variety of diagnostic tests have also been produced which provide useful information for teachers.

Similarly, developments have also occurred in the approaches used for the formal assessment of pupils with SEN. Despite legitimate criticisms of the assessment approaches adopted by the SATs and GCSE courses, there is evidence of a greater flexibility for pupils, particularly those with learning difficulties. Extra time for reading the questions, the taping of question papers, the use of readers and writers has helped to aid some pupils to be able to better demonstrate their knowledge and understanding of what they have learned.

CONCLUSIONS

For much of the past hundred years the provision and resources available for pupils with SEN has been inadequate to meet the needs of many of the pupils so categorised. Changes in legislation have often been under-resourced or lacking in any financial input at government level. This situation has led to wide-ranging criticisms of provision for children with SEN in mainstream schools.

However, developments can be identified in a number of areas which have helped teachers who are working with children with SEN. Such developments can be identified in relation to assessment strategies to better identify pupils and determine their learning needs. This has been accompanied by the gradual development of more appropriate teaching and learning materials for children with SEN. Recently professionally published materials of a more appropriate reading age and interest level have become available. Nevertheless, an analysis of the evidence shows that the commitment to resource SEN provision continues to be inadequate and is a source of frustration to those working in this area.

Societal influences

INTRODUCTION

The acceptability of children with SEN in mainstream schools is dependent on a wide range of considerations. Among the most important of these is the attitude that is displayed towards them by the able-bodied, the structures which are put in place to help them actively participate in school life and the degree of influence and control which their advocates have. Since the introduction of compulsory schooling, tensions can be identified which have led to disputes and difficulties over the best way to address the problems of pupils with SEN and to accommodate them within the wider society. However much legislation is passed by Parliament and resources made available to provide educational opportunities for children with SEN, the crucial factor is their social acceptance and participation in the wider society. This chapter will concentrate on an analysis of these issues.

BACKGROUND

Attitudes to people with disabilities in society, regardless of their age, are not static, rather they are constantly changing. Despite criticisms by Green (1968) over the pace of change in the UK compared with other countries, British society has been described by Halsey (1978) as one of 'continuity and change'. The school is regarded as a key element in this process, therefore developments which have taken place with regard to provision for pupils with SEN can be reasonably regarded as a reflection of the changing attitudes within society as a whole towards the disabled.

Kogan (1978) argued that the purposes and procedures of education reflect the wishes of people in society. He suggested that this produces an essentially conflicting model based on assertions and reconciliation of negotiations as part of an overall debate. In this respect there is an inextricable link between educational, social and political processes.

Weber (1978) and Ranson (1994) have argued that this process is based on an essentially tripartite model of organisation, relating to the control of power in society. Ranson (1994) links this process to the key features of organising principles, the socio-constitutive system and social power structures in a society. This is shown in more detail in Figure 2.

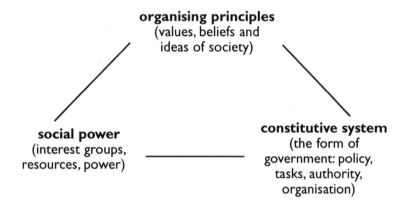

organising principles
(values, beliefs and
ideas of society)

social power
(interest groups,
resources, power)

constitutive system
(the form of
government: policy,
tasks, authority,
organisation)

Figure 2: A model of power and organisation in education (based on Ranson 1994, p. 11)

For those working with pupils with SEN this is a particularly valuable model for understanding the conflicting interests involved in the difficulties regarding SEN that have arisen over the years. These have manifested themselves in a variety of ways. Those relating to the constitutive system and social power have been discussed in earlier chapters of this book. This chapter will focus particularly on aspects relating to the organising principles in society and the effect of its overarching values and beliefs on children with SEN.

There is considerable reason to believe, following the work of the Schools' Council (1970, 1971) the Snowdon Report (1976) and research by Tomlinson (1982) Ford (1982), and Humphreys and Gordon (1992) that many children with disabilities have long felt discriminated against by both their peers and their teachers during their period of formal schooling. This has resulted in a feeling, for some at least, of being stigmatised by the society. This has taken many guises relating both to their acceptability in society and their accessibility to it.

Humphreys and Gordon (1992) indicated that this has led to some children with SEN being labelled and categorised as unworthy and incapable, often both academically and socially. This has contributed to feelings of low self esteem and consequently had an effect on their level of frustration and anger that has inhibited their personal development.

In some respects this is an issue clearly allied to full integration within society of people with disabilities. It is important, however, that this is discussed within the wider societal context in order to illustrate the background issues that have led to pressures for change in the education of children with SEN during the past century.

It is often hard for young people with disabilities, particularly those with learning difficulties, to campaign for change on their own behalf. Children with dyslexia or those with communication problems often have relatively fewer means of doing this or have difficulties in having their problems accepted. Often their key advocates have been their parents, who in this respect, throughout the years of compulsory schooling, have played a highly influential role in initiating change. It is these parents who have often written letters or campaigned for change in the education system. This has not been an easy task. Another theme of this chapter is to discuss the effect that their activities have had in bringing about changes for their children in the educational system.

Changes brought about in educational provision for children with SEN as a result of societal pressures can be seen to have two sources. The first results from focusing directly on the needs and aspirations of children with SEN. An example of this is the developments that have taken place relating to the greater integration of pupils with SEN into mainstream schools. The second source of change in SEN provision occurs through developments that have taken place as a result of change in the wider educational context. An example of this in recent years is the development of the National Curriculum, which has affected all pupils of compulsory school age. A historical analysis indicates there are a number of key issues of importance in this respect. These include: the development of comprehensive education, the raising of the school leaving age and the greater prevalence of mixed ability teaching. Each of these factors has had an effect on provision for children with SEN.

A PLACE IN SOCIETY

Pritchard (1963), Cole (1989, 1990) and Hurt (1988) have identified a compassionate and essentially humanistic approach to children with SEN as the main perspective taken by society over the years. There is evidence of many individual examples of developments in SEN provision which have been driven by compassion. Those who founded schools for the disabled, those who provided charity for their upkeep and those who worked on behalf of the rights of disabled people can be counted in this group.

Tomlinson (1982) and Ford (1982) however, have argued that an analysis based on compassionate and humanistic motives was too simplistic. They suggest that society has little sympathy for the disabled, particularly those with severe problems. In their view, the overriding concern of society at large has focused on the part those with disabilities could play in national economic and commercial strategies. It seems likely that both compassionate and economic influences have been important in bringing about change.

Humphries and Gordon (1992) described the situation for people with disabilities as being one in which they are treated with fear, embarrassment and even disgust by the able-bodied in society and suggest that they are often treated in an uncaring, patronising way in a harsh and hostile world.

Perhaps surprisingly, this has also been found to be the case with religious groups involved in working with people with disabilities, from whom a more positive spirit would have been expected. Tomlinson (1982) indicated that for many religious groups involved with disabled people, particularly those influenced by the Protestant ethic, developments were based on economic rather than charitable motives. The important goal for these groups was seen as the development of self-sufficiency, so that as adults they would not have to rely on financial handouts. Although by contemporary standards this attitude is perhaps unexpected, it is in some ways hardly surprising in that Luther himself considered that people with disabilities were 'Godless'.

Many children with SEN, until comparatively recently, were brought up in a world of ignorance, fear and superstition. The view that families were punished by God by being given a sickly child persisted well into the present century. This was seen as a form of divine retribution for the wickedness of man, a feature in some cultures which could be applied to the individual. In some families, until the advent of improved medical care and changes in the attitude of society to the disabled, when a deformity was clear at birth the doctor, midwife or sometimes even parents themselves would sometimes conspire to allow the baby to die.

For other children, ignorance was more of a social or medical problem. Poverty, poor housing, a lack of health care and non-existent sanitation meant that many were left exposed to disease. Humphrey and Gordon (1992) calculated that in the period before the outbreak of war in 1939, in the larger cities, many large families had at least one child with a disability. In some cases these disabilities were clearly evident from birth, for example: blindness, deafness and hereditary rickets. Others like polio and TB were commonplace in infancy. In other cases, through environmental, locational and hereditary factors, such difficulties did not manifest themselves until children reached school age and could not cope with the work that was expected of them.

The mid-nineteenth century witnessed the development of an ethos in society towards what has been described as 'muscular Christianity'. The key values of this have been described by Walvin (1995) as part of the Victorian preoccupation with a healthy and beautiful body. Further, it was associated with the concept of wholesomeness with regard particularly to masculinity, physical strength and fitness. This was a movement supported at the turn of the century through the influence of organisations such as the Boy Scouts and the Church Lads Brigade. Equivalents for girls, and the attributes of feminism, can be found in the Girl Guides. This ideology was founded on the concepts of imperialism and national supremacy, through the power of the armed forces which perceived Britain as the supreme world power and 'ruling the waves'.

Humphries and Gordon (1992) argued that forms of stereotyping caused serious difficulties for the disabled in society, and also for their parents. To have fathered such a child was regarded in some quarters as an indication of a lack of masculinity. For mothers it was a source of shame and failure. As a consequence of this disabled children were often hidden, rarely left the family home and were sometimes shunned by their parents. This was reported to be particularly the case with fathers who could sometimes completely disown such children.

THE EUGENICS MOVEMENT

The position of children with SEN in society was heightened in the early part of the present century through the influence of the Eugenics Movement which came to prominence in 1907. Tomlinson (1982) highlighted the importance of the influence of this group on not only contemporary provision and organisation but to a lesser extent for much of the inter-war period also.

The views of the Eugenicists were radical as well as largely negative in many respects. They were set around concepts and prejudices based on the ignorance, confusion and fear that surrounded Victorian medical knowledge of mental illness as well as on ideas of selective breeding that, it was argued, would lead to an overall improvement in the performance of the human race.

The more radical Eugenicists argued strongly that the only way forward for the benefit of society as a whole was for the eradication of the disabilities from which people suffered. This, they argued, should be best done through children with such problems being housed separately in institutions so that their lives could be deliberately controlled in order to prevent regeneration. Also, there was a deliberate policy of sterilisation of certain disability groups to prevent reproduction in a number of states in the USA.

It was the attitudes of this wing of the movement that emerged later in Nazi Germany where there was for some years a policy of extermination for the weak and handicapped. Figures indicate that between 1938 and 1941 some 70 000 disabled children in Germany were exterminated in death camps because of this policy. In Britain, some members of the Eugenics group from the turn of the century onwards had argued that no form of educational provision should be made for such children.

The less radical wing of the Eugenics group argued that those who had disabilities should be deliberately placed in separate villages or colonies in rural settings This, they thought, was particularly appropriate for the low grade feeble-minded. Again, the idea was to control their lives and thereby prevent sexual relationships developing which might continue the defect into a further generation.

The influence of this group was substantial in the period leading up to the First World War period. One member of the group, while giving evidence to the Royal Commission on the Care and Control of Feeble Minded in 1908, declared that such children were 'social rubbish'. Mary Dendy, the founder of an institution for children with disabilities in Cheshire, claimed to have examined 40 000 Manchester schoolchildren and told the Commissioners in 1905 that all the 220 children in the special school classes in the city should be segregated as they were a 'definite risk to society'.

Tredgold (1908) whose book on mental deficiency was of considerable influence on educational provision at the time, was an enthusiastic supporter of the Eugenics movement. Giving evidence to the Royal Commission in 1908, he described the mildly feeble-minded as 'swelling the ranks of the insane'.

The question of sanity was only one factor in the minds of some of this group. Poor intelligence and social handicap were closely linked for some to crime and low living. Much of the basis for this was from the work of Galton (1869) who had concluded that there was a hereditary base for intelligence and for criminal tendencies. In the early part of the twentieth century this view was supported by the work of Dugdale (1877) and Goddard (1912) who linked poor intelligence to unemployment and prostitution as well as criminal tendencies.

Despite the influence of the Eugenicists, there were opposing voices who put the case for a more considered approach to those who were in need of special provision. One of the most influential of these was the Chief Medical Officer of Health of the time who, in giving evidence to the Royal Commission (1908), stated that many of the children so maligned by the Eugenics Movement were educable. He argued that the craze for scientific officialdom and social experimentation was acting as a trap for them.

A DEPENDENCY CULTURE

The concept of dependency was a key factor in the period before the introduction of the welfare state. It was an overwhelming view of society that children should be trained for work and prepared for a role in society. As has been the overall philosophy generally throughout the period, the concept of independence underpinned both philosophical and practical approaches. Where the nature of the disability allowed it was expected that children, on leaving school, would go out to work to earn a living and contribute to the family budget. From time to time this has led to conflict between school and parents.

One example of this arose in the nineteenth century when there was considerable pressure to extend the period of compulsory schooling for those in special education. For some families, where the children were receiving their education in special schools, and there was a chance that they would get employment after leaving, some parents resented the extra compulsory year as it prevented them from being able to contribute to the family budget during that time. This was an important factor in some poorer families where an extra wage packet would be a considerable help. For many, however, employment prospects were much more difficult or even impossible. Post school activities often took the form of continued training in a situation that had neither status nor financial reward for those undertaking this.

The present situation where employment prospects are more difficult for all school leavers has not helped the prospects of young people with SEN. Beyond this there is greater employer expectation of children undertaking external examinations. As such, the situation for children with SEN has deteriorated further. In an increasingly technologically driven world the days of the unskilled worker have all but disappeared, removing many of the jobs traditionally done by young people with learning difficulties. For those for whom this is a reality, they have been described by Humphries and Gordon (1992) as an underclass neglected by society and denied realistic opportunities in the world of work. The consequence of this for motivating pupils with SEN to do well at school has yet to be adequately addressed.

Tomlinson (1982) indicated that for many children with SEN the focus of schooling is not on educational achievement or a job. Rather, it is on social control. She argued that one of the hallmarks of success for children with SEN is their ability to fit inobtrusively into adult society, where a degree of social compliance is essential.

LABELLING

The terminology used to describe pupils with SEN in the education system is an indicator of the changing attitudes in society. This is the case especially for pupils with learning difficulties. That there were different levels of difficulties has long been clear to those working in the field, but there has been little consistency of language to describe these levels.

The nineteenth century terminology was, by current standards, both crude and bleak. By the standards of the late twentieth century it was also severely prejudicial. Words such as idiot, imbecile, feeble-minded, defective and lunatic were the common contemporary descriptions in both official and vernacular usage. This was the terminology of the asylum. Pritchard (1963) and Cohen and Cohen (1986) outlined the history of these terms and pointed out that by the early part of the nineteenth century their meanings had become blurred and interchangeable. Beyond this these terms were a pertinent reflection of the lack of respect that society held for those who were so described.

Yet these children were to be found in considerable numbers, exhibiting a considerable variety in their personal needs. It was the advent of compulsory schooling in 1880 that exposed them far more to public awareness and placed them in an education system that was not capable of coping with their difficulties and needs. Even by the beginning of the present century there was little special provision in the mainstream school for children with disabilities.

The need to categorise and describe children with difficulties in school has a long history. Throughout the whole period of compulsory education it has been seen as a necessary but difficult task. The Egerton Commission (1889) made some attempt to rationalise the terminology and to provide a working definition of the categories used for children with SEN. In the event, this was not very useful since each of the categories outlined was set in relative values and the others within a deficit model. Idiots were defined as having a greater deficiency of intellect of the two categories, while the imbecile had a lesser degree of such a deficiency. In educational terms these definitions were somewhat crude. For example, the group defined as imbeciles were considered to be educable in relation to physical training rather than reading, writing or arithmetic.

It was not until the Sharpe Committee (1896) that any real attempt was made to sort out clearly defined terms to describe these categories. Significantly, the new definitions created were based as much on socio-economic as educational factors. In a reflection of the values current in society as a whole, pupils were defined in terms of their level of dependency on the rest of society as much as their educational difficulties or needs.

The key words used in the Sharpe Report (1896) were imbecile and feeble-minded. It defined an imbecile as someone who could not be educated to a level where they could become self-supporting. The feeble-minded were those who were too weak mentally to gain much benefit from school, but who were not too incapable of looking after themselves with a degree of independence.

In the final analysis, however, the Committee balked at this terminology, disliking the term feeble-minded and substituting the term 'defective'. The label defective was used as an umbrella term to describe pupils with either physical or mental difficulties and persisted up to the time of the 1944 Education Act.

In the inter-war period little was done which was of lasting value. The certification introduced for those in need of special school education in 1921 only increased feelings of separation and the stigma attached to this group of children. This was also true for the parents of such children who regarded special schools in very negative terms and were generally angered by the labelling of their children in this way.

The Wood Report (1929), set up to help clarify thinking and to produce an overall national policy in this area, had little immediate influence on the situation, although some of its recommendations had a considerable impact in the immediate post-war period.

STIGMA

Criticisms of the 1921 Education Act were renewed at the time of the Wood Report (1929). The problems over certification were unresolved and little was done to provide any real direction for future policy regarding children with SEN. Tansley and Gulliford (1960) condemned the report in terms of producing a long-lasting stigma for those pupils who attended special school and who, as a consequence of this, were regarded as abnormal. Tomlinson (1982), perhaps understating the situation, commented that parents remained unenthusiastic about the situation.

This stigma was accentuated by the requirement of the 1921 Act for the certification of all children in special schools. Further, although indicating the broad categories of pupils needing help, from the teachers' point of view, it gave little guidance as to how this might be provided, either by means of the overall strategies or through the ability of individual teachers to provide programmes of work for such pupils.

In the inter-war period the teachers' unions continued to be favourable to the exclusion of certain children from the education system. As opposition grew in other quarters on the certification issue some were opposed to its abolition. Teachers in special schools were particularly against the abolition of certification, perhaps for the pragmatic reason that they may lose pupils and perhaps face unemployment.

FORMAL CATEGORISATION

After the end of the Second World War in 1945 there was a desire for change throughout the whole country and educational provision was at its forefront. The initial planning for these changes had been set out in the late 1930s through the Hadow Report (1926) and the Spens Report (1938), which covered both primary and secondary phases of provision.

The major thrust of the 1944 Act was the introduction of compulsory secondary education. However, within the Act there were also considerable changes regarding pupils with SEN as part of a strong political will for change and to make better provision for all children. The 1944 Education Act was seen at the time as an answer to many of the questions and difficulties relating to both overall policy and the sort of provision to be made for children with SEN. The challenge was to ensure that the mistakes over the categorisation, and consequent stigmatisation of special education in the previous Act of

Parliament was not repeated.

The aim for pupils with SEN was to set out a framework which would avoid these difficulties. This framework, which again involved discreet categories of pupils and in fact increased these, lasted almost 40 years until the implementation of the 1981 Education Act in April 1983. Categorisation of children with SEN was seen as an important component of the 1944 Education Act. It was seen as an aid to the development of provision. By defining carefully the various groups of pupils and their difficulties, it was argued that correct provision could be made for them and the previous rather haphazard approach could be improved.

Three features of the 1944 Act were of major importance in this respect. Firstly, all local education authorities were required to make provision for children with SEN, wherever possible within mainstream schools. Secondly, through the language used in the discussions about the passing of the Act through Parliament and the subsequent documentation, the concept of special education was introduced to indicate those pupils to which the relevant sections were targeted. This was defined in terms of the methods used to help such children and in relation to the provision which was made for them.

Thirdly, in the Act the phrase special educational treatment is used to refer to all children with disabilities, whether in separate special schools or within the mainstream system. This was an important feature which was to form an integral part of the initial thinking of the Warnock Committee some 30 years later in an attempt to construct a unified concept of provision.

Subsequently to the 1944 Act the Handicapped Pupils and Health Service Regulations (1945) defined eleven categories of handicap. Two of these (maladjustment and speech defective) were new legislative categories, and with the exception of the category for the diabetic, which was incorporated into the delicate category in 1953, these categories remained an important part of the outline framework for special educational provision until the 1981 Education Act.

Further, these regulations emphasised that with the exception of those children who were defined as seriously handicapped (the blind, deaf, epileptic, physically handicapped and aphasic) all could attend the mainstream school, should adequate provision be available to them.

This point was further emphasised through the guidance issued by the Department of Education (1946) which indicated that pupils in the 'sub-normal' category (defined as children who were retarded) should be educated in mainstream schools.

INCLUSION

By the early 1970s the formal categories set out in the 1945 regulations were seen to have lost their value. By then they were often viewed as unhelpful, setting up barriers and a hindrance to pupils with difficulties. Within the social context of change prevalent at the time it was thought that these were no longer immediately relevant to contemporary social circumstances. The evidence presented to the Warnock Committee (1978) reflected these changes. The subsequent 1981 Act along with the Education (Special Educational Needs) Regulation (1983) attempted to transform these views into a legal framework.

The definition of provision was changed radically through the direction of the Warnock Report (1978) and the 1981 Act. The emphasis was on inclusion and a far more individual child-centred approach rather than on forms of categorisation. Essentially the philosophical emphasis moved to attempting to provide access for pupils both in a physical and a social sense. The HMI/Audit Commission Report (1992) indicated however that there continued to be considerable variations in provision in different parts of the country and to some extent old attitudes continued to persist.

Changes which were made did not come quickly enough in some areas, and were not radical enough in others. Nevertheless, the overall changes which have been introduced during the last few years have generally been welcomed by those staff working in the field, the pupils and their parents. It would be naive, and clearly wrong, to indicate a feeling of general satisfaction over the work which has been done. Certainly the circumstances are better now than ever before but there is hardly room for complacency.

The philosophy behind the introduction of the National Curriculum in 1989 again has promoted inclusion although, in practical terms the value of its impact is much more doubtful as it made few separate provisions for pupils with SEN. The concept of a curriculum programme for all pupils argued for in the Warnock Report (1978) was enshrined in the 1988 Education Act. In this respect the issue is now the level of appropriate work for individual children and their pace of learning rather than a separation of provision.

ALLIED DEVELOPMENTS IN SCHOOL

The changes which took place as a consequence of the 1944 Education Act, as far as pupils with SEN were concerned, have to be taken in conjunction with the changes which occurred throughout the whole of secondary school provision. The basis of this was that outlined in the Spens Report and further discussed in the Norwood Report (1943).

Across the country the provision which was available was far from uniform. In fact there was then, as there is now, a considerable variety of different forms of provision available. These differences included the adoption of the complete tripartite system of provision in some LEAs, with grammar, technical and modern schools. In many authorities only the grammar and modern schools were built, while others had bilateral schools and a few decided to build some 'all-in' comprehensive schools.

However, it is possible to identify three crucial areas where developments occurred which have led to changes in the lives of many pupils with SEN in mainstream secondary schools. These are: the development of comprehensive education, the rise in mixed ability classes and the raising of the school leaving age to 16 in 1973.

Comprehensive education

Despite all the debate leading up to the introduction of the 1944 Act about the form of provision most suitable for secondary education in England and Wales, there was soon considerable doubt about the tripartite system of grammar, technical and secondary modern schools which was adopted.

Criticisms were raised in the early 1950s about the inflexibility of the system. Some of these were concerned with the fact that decisions were made about children's education at the age of 11 which, in most cases, were irreversible. Another criticism was that the modern school was seen as second rate and in some LEAs third rate. The lack of any recognised form of externally recognised examination for school leavers was also seen as a weakness of the secondary modern school in particular. Very soon after inception this approach to secondary schooling was seen as reinforcing self-fulfilling prophecies by many parents and teachers.

Pedley (1963), Musgrave (1968) and Lawson and Silver (1973) provided considerable evidence of growing support among politicians and other influential parties for a more egalitarian approach and a genuine quality secondary education for all. By the early 1970s this included at least some who regarded the 'all' to include pupils with SEN. Pedley (1963) argued that reforms of this nature would aid the development of more satisfactory educational opportunities through better staffing and organisational flexibility. He also argued that curriculum provision would also be improved and benefit all pupils if a system of comprehensive schools was widely adopted. His point was that the size of these schools and the number of staff within them would allow the curriculum to be constructed around the individual needs of pupils, which would particularly suit children with SEN.

Government circular 10/65 demanded that all LEAs must prepare plans to introduce comprehensive secondary education in their area. This was a move which was rescinded after the change of government in 1970 which led to a chaotic situation in which some LEAs maintained comprehensive schools, others had kept grammar schools and some even had both.

Writing with the hindsight of experience, Booth (1981) pointed out that despite the hopes of some reformers, the comprehensive school was far from a haven of tolerance for pupils needing special help. This point was further underlined by Holt (1964),and restated by Hargreaves (1967, 1982), Sumner and Warburton (1972), Rutter (1975), Willis (1977) and Stakes (1986). Ford (1982) described the comprehensive school as pernicious for such pupils as it did not allow them to exert their full freedom of choice there.

This was a point supported by Woods (1978), while Willis (1977) argued that a major flaw in the comprehensive system was that many pupils who were not academically inclined were unable to take any formal examinations and as such felt increasingly sidelined within mainstream schools (Hodgson *et al* 1984). Willis (1977) found that many older pupils felt they had outgrown school, regarding it as a place for 'kids' and a crèche for adolescents. It was for them a preparation for adulthood which had failed.

The reasons for this state of affairs are discussed elsewhere in this book but the continued prominence of the debate over the value of the comprehensive school is indicative of an underlying concern over this form of provision for pupils with SEN. It is a much wider debate than the effectiveness of provision for pupils with SEN, however the unsuitability of many of the curriculum programmes for the less capable pupils must be taken into account.

Mixed Ability Teaching
The development of the comprehensive secondary school brought with it a growth of mixed ability teaching, similar to that commonly found in primary schools after the publication of the Plowden Report (1965). One of the consequences of this was that children with SEN found themselves placed for much of their timetabled time in teaching groups with their more academically and socially successful peers. Such changes needed considerable planning and organisational skills in order for them to be successful. However, there was little

experience of this among staff and considerable doubt among many of them as to its value. Critics (for example the contributors to the Black papers on Education (1969, 1970)) saw this as less of an educational move and more related to social engineering.

Evidence from contemporary literature indicates that, although this move was welcomed in theory by many parents, pupils with SEN and their teachers, it presented considerable practical difficulties for the pupils. Gulliford (1969) argued that mixed ability teaching, although perhaps helping to alleviate some social difficulties among pupils with SEN, presented further problems such as the lack of specialised staff available to help them succeed in this new situation.

Similar criticisms were raised in official reports. The Bullock Report (1975) described the complexity of mixed ability teaching as considerable. Brennan (1979) and HMI (1979), in widely recognised national surveys, were sceptical of this form of provision, certainly as far as the less able were concerned. In both of these studies teams of observers indicated that they had not encountered any mixed ability teaching in which the curricular needs of pupils with SEN were being met satisfactorily.

An NFER survey (1976) found that staff were facing difficulties in relation to classroom management skills. The difficulties of working with the least able pupils were among those most commonly raised by the 400 teachers who were interviewed. The most common issues which were raised were how the teacher could best provide for these children, in what ways could specialist help be provided to aid the class teacher and those pupils in greatest need and what resources, materials and teaching techniques were most appropriate for this group.

These problems were further complicated by discussions regarding the form of organisational structure to provide the best provision for children with SEN in conjunction with that which was the best for the rest of the pupils. Clunies-Ross *et al* (1983), in a major survey of organisational strategies for pupils with SEN in mainstream schools, detailed some of the dilemmas. These included: difficulties about who should have the day-to-day responsibility for pupils with SEN, the possible level of integration for pupils within the mainstream school, the best approach to developing the skills of teachers working with pupils with SEN, the extent of the specialist teacher's role as an advisor within the school and the development of appropriate lines of communication, both within the school and outside it, to strengthen links with outside professionals and agencies.

A number of departmental heads confronted with these issues wrote about some of their difficulties. Benger (1971) was concerned about meeting the needs of individual pupils, the danger of the time available being wasted, and the timetable difficulties due to the lack of participation which any of the less able pupils had in the more academic subjects. Cornell (1974) described his school's approach to overcoming such difficulties through team teaching, which was co-ordinated by a senior member of staff. Watts (1976) argued that this approach provided a totally integrated approach for all pupils who needed special help alongside the rest of their peer group in many of their subject areas right through to school leaving age at sixteen. Similar organisational arrangements were outlined by Williams (1969) and Gordon and Wilson (1979) and involved the use of withdrawal groups and resource bases.

The essential difficulty, however, remained one of balancing the social benefits of mixed ability teaching for pupils with SEN with the emotional and behavioural problems which they can sometimes exhibit. Booth (1981) described such a situation as one of ambiguity and summed up the situation as one where, although alleviating some of the constraints and pressures, it nevertheless produced its own in trying to cater for the interests of a diverse group of pupils. As with the debate on comprehensive schooling it is a dispute which continues and which recently has taken on a considerably more prominent political dimension.

The Raising of the School Leaving Age (ROSLA)
The school leaving age for all pupils has gradually been raised throughout the period of compulsory schooling in England and Wales. The most recent change was to raise it to the age of 16 in 1973. This meant an extra year at school for all pupils.

This change had major implications for those pupils with SEN. One of these was that a suitable curriculum needed to be planned for such pupils in their final years at secondary school. In particular it saw the development of courses in the last two years of compulsory schooling which were more appropriate for pupils with SEN. Some of these were organised as separate bolt-on courses while others were based on a variety of cross curricular initiatives. Social Studies and Environmental Studies programmes were good examples of these. Increasingly these courses had recognised examinations at sixteen available for pupils. These examinations, of which the Certificate of Secondary Education (CSE) were the most common, caused problems in that they were often set at an inappropriate academic level for children with learning difficulties and still left them with little incentive to work in their final years of compulsory education. These developments were discussed by McNicholas (1979) and were based on his own experience of trying to organise and teach such courses in his own school.

Other courses were organised with the express intention of placing the least successful pupils with the rest of their peer group in a wider academic setting. Brennan (1979) in a survey of successful courses, gave some examples of those which were available. These included courses in parenthood, social studies and humanities. Examples of courses organised in individual schools were described by Rogers (1971, 1973) and Watts (1978).

The literature indicates that these developments placed the staff involved in organising such courses in a new and wider context. Some of them were taught by the individual departments responsible for the less able, while others were organised on a co-operative inter-departmental basis. It was this latter arrangement which helped to place the SEN specialist in a new situation amongst their colleagues (bringing them 'out of the broom-cupboard', as it was put at the time). It was this development which helped to place them in a more advisory capacity amongst their colleagues, and a situation which helped in engendering a new role and a new status for SEN within the school.

PARENTAL INVOLVEMENT

The 1981 Education Act provided for the first time a legal framework for the involvement of parents of children with SEN in the education of their children. Despite the evidence of Fraser (1959), Floud, Halsey and Martin (1956), Douglas (1964), Douglas *et al* (1971), Jackson and Marsden (1962) and Craft, Raynor and Cohen (1967), which indicated the overall importance of parental involvement in relation to the success of a child in school, there is overwhelming evidence to show that parents were, until relatively recently, not really seen as partners in their children's education by teachers. Parental interest was often regarded as interference and questions and enquiries were seen as unhelpful.

Green (1968) indicated this well when describing some contemporary common practices. One of his examples included a line drawn across a school playground stating 'no parents beyond this point'. Midwinter (1974), when discussing the importance of this relationship to the success of the child in school, suggested it was often one of the school educating the child, and home having to get in where it could. Gleidman and Roth (1981) saw it as a moral issue, arguing that, except in the most extreme of cases, teachers have no right to use their power to intimidate or manipulate.

The benefits of involving parents in their children's education first gained widespread acknowledgement from teachers in the 1960s following the publication of the Plowden Report (DES 1967) and reports on projects conducted on educational priority areas, most of which involved working closely with parents. Wolfendale (1993) indicated that legislation enacted in the last fifteen years has had the effect of increasing the importance of parental involvement in education since parents' rights have been extended.

Through the 1980 Education Act parents were granted the right to choose the school they wanted to send their children to. Parents were also given the right to be represented on the governing bodies of schools. In addition, school governors and LEAs was required to provide written information to parents on admission criteria, the curriculum, examination results, the discipline policy and school organisation.

The 1981 Education Act contained many of the recommendations of the Warnock Report (DES 1978). It was solely concerned with children with SEN. The Warnock Committee (1978) argued that the necessary relationship must be set in more clearly formal, even legal, terms. This, at least in part, was carried through into the 1981 Education Act. For parents of children with special needs the Warnock Committee's recommendations were a crucial development. The Report concluded that these children and their parents must be seen as partners, both with the school and other agencies involved in the provision which might be made. It was evident to the Committee that the position of parents would be consolidated, if not strengthened, from that outlined in the 1944 Act.

The 1981 Act gave parents the right to request the LEA to conduct a formal assessment of their children's special educational needs. It requires parental involvement in the assessment process and in rigor mortis of their children's progress. It also gives parents the right to appeal against LEA decisions about their children. Further, it made it clear that parents' wishes should be taken into account when deciding whether or not to integrate children with SEN into ordinary schools.

The first of two Education Acts in 1986 required increased parental representation on the governing bodies of schools. Governors were required to present an annual report to parents and to have a meeting with parents at the school in order to discuss it.

The 1988 Act granted parents the right to send their children to any school of their choice so long as it has room to accommodate them. It also requires that parents are sent an annual report of their children's progress. In addition, it gave schools the opportunity of opting out of

LEA control if a majority of parents voted in favour of this.

New procedures for the inspection of schools were set out in the 1992 Education Act, giving parents an increased role. Parents have the right to meet with the inspectors before the inspection to discuss any issues they wish. School staff and governors are not allowed to be present unless the children attend the school. Also all parents are sent a questionnaire by the inspectors asking for their comments on the school. In addition, inspectors are expected to have discussions with parents on a wide range of issues concerning the school. These include: the way that parents are involved in the identification and assessment of SEN and the annual review of statements. Parents also have the right to receive a summary report of the results of school inspections.

The Code of Practice (1994) which also provides guidance on the implementation of the 1993 Act, emphasises the importance for schools of establishing partnerships with parents. It requires schools to be active in three respects. Firstly, schools should have a written policy and procedure for SEN; secondly, they must provide parents with information and thirdly, they must allow parents access to information.

The written policy and procedures should include: a policy for acting on parental concerns, the arrangements for involving parents when teachers express concerns about their child and arrangements for incorporating parents' views in the assessment procedure and the reviews of progress.

Information should be supplied on the school policy for SEN, the support and services available within both the school and the LEA for children with SEN, parents' rights to be involved in the assessment and decision-making process and names of voluntary organisations that can provide guidance and support.

Information for parents should be provided in the community language spoken by parents. Information should be provided on audio tape for parents with literacy difficulties and a parents' room or other arrangements should be provided to help parents feel comfortable about coming to school.

The effect of the 1993 Education Act should be to further strengthen parental influence over the education of their children. The increasing emphasis on parents' rights that has evolved through recent legislation means that schools must work closely with parents. The emphasis on positive parental involvement that is embodied in the Code of Practice (1994) is indicative of the considerable progress which there has been in societal attitudes towards parental involvement in the hundred years since compulsory schooling began. The challenge now is to ensure that the practice of parental involvement matches the principles that are agreed. At the moment the practice of parental involvement varies markedly from school to school and from teacher to teacher. Progress for children with SEN will be supported by policies for involving parents being implemented consistently on a much wider scale than is presently the case.

CONCLUSIONS

The attitudes displayed towards children with SEN by the able-bodied in society has had a major impact on their acceptance within mainstream schools. Attempts to help the educational development of children with SEN have often been well intentioned but from a practical point of view they have often been a source of frustration to children with SEN. Seemingly good ideas such as the categories of disability detailed in the various Education Acts or the use of streamed classes in schools have, in the longer term, been unhelpful to children with SEN and have sometimes led to blatant prejudice. Changes in recent years, through the influence of the Warnock Report (1978) in particular, with views on the greater access to facilities offered in mainstream schools have helped. Further, developments in schools and a generally more sympathetic approach both by staff and society, have helped to create a more positive climate.

Although children with SEN have received compassion and sympathy collectively there is evidence of a lack of value of their contribution to society. Society has tended to dismiss their usefulness and treat them as second class citizens. Throughout the century many children with SEN have been treated with embarrassment and contempt. There has been a lack of thrust regarding their greater integration into society. Difficulties over their economic usefulness as adults continues to be heightened by the general lack of suitable employment for them at school leaving age.

Children with disabilities, regardless of their age, often have considerable difficulties in speaking out on their own behalf. Pressure groups formed by parents and supported by their teachers have often been important allies in increasing fuller participation for children with SEN in society. Over the past twenty years this has led to an increase in parental legal rights. From this point of view their pressure has brought about some benefits. However, if some of these changes are not to remain merely cosmetic there must be continued vigilance to ensure that all children, regardless of their disabilities, are unquestionably accepted in society and given the same educational opportunities as the rest of their peers.

Towards an appropriate curriculum

INTRODUCTION

The contents of the school curriculum in the UK throughout much of this century has been largely uncontroversial. Throughout this time curriculum content has generally been left in the hands of individual schools and the classroom teacher has had enormous influence on what has been taught to individual children. This was the case particularly between the end of the period of formal government control of the curriculum in 1924 and the introduction of the National Curriculum in 1988. In that time the only compulsory subject was Religious Education.

Discussions on the curriculum have concentrated essentially on the level of knowledge and skill pupils should acquire from their experiences of school. For pupils with SEN, until the time of the introduction of the National Curriculum (1988) this essentially liberal approach to curriculum content enabled the adoption of a largely child-centred approach to their learning. Since its introduction, the National Curriculum has provided much tighter guidelines on what should be taught to pupils with SEN. The introduction of Standard Assessment Tests (SATs), OFSTED inspections and the publication of league tables of external examination results have also had an effect on how pupils are taught and assessed.

Taking these factors into account, this chapter will discuss issues relating to changes in the selection of the curriculum as well as its management for pupils with SEN. Particular issues which will be discussed include: the purpose of the curriculum, its choice and content, appropriate curriculum models for children with SEN and the models which are available to deliver these as well as the effect of the introduction of the National Curriculum on pupils with SEN.

CONTENT

Decisions relating to the content of the school curriculum for pupils with SEN are not easy to resolve. For many years it was considered that separate curricula were appropriate for most children with special needs. The thinking of the Warnock Committee (1978) with its views on 'a curriculum for all' acted as an important influence on later practice. The introduction of the National Curriculum only served to firm up this position. In recent years there has been a moratorium on change in the content of the National Curriculum. Nevertheless, the debate over its value for pupils with SEN continues.

Bernstein (1971) described the contents of the school curriculum as valid knowledge which pupils should know, be taught or experience. Hirst and Peters (1970) and Solstis (1968) viewed curriculum content as a fluid concept, with varying perceptions about what constitutes an educated person. Williams (1958) argued that the purpose of education has three inter-related aspects. These are concerned with training children in the values and acceptable behaviour patterns of society, the acquisition of general knowledge and attitudes and thirdly the teaching of skills that will enable them to earn a living and make a contribution to the welfare of society.

To Peters (1967, 1983) this was too narrow a definition. He argued that the concept of education and thus the curriculum programme must take into account aspects such as knowledge, understanding, judgement and feelings, and not be confined to utilitarian and vocational issues. It is the development of the individual in this context that, in his view, produces the educated person.

It is these two conflicting viewpoints of the purposes of education: to help one fit into a place in society on the one hand, or education to promote one's own personal development that presents the greatest problem. This is particularly the case for pupils with SEN. This group is often the least proactive in either of these areas. It is arguable that from the former perspective they are often likely to end up in the worst possible circumstances in society while in the latter they often have so few powers of self advocacy and personal influence that they have to rely on the good intentions of others to promote their interests.

CURRICULUM MODELS

A short survey of the key models that have developed over the century provides some understanding of the difficulties that exist for many pupils with SEN. This can best be done through providing an insight into the most used curriculum approaches for all pupils.

These are the essentialist, the encylopaedic and the pragmatic and the discovery models; all of which continue to influence the curricular programme offered in schools for children of all abilities.

Essentialism
The essentialist model of the curriculum is based on the theory of Plato, which regards the teacher as having an essentially political role. He argued that the aim of education was to sustain a just society. This, in his view, must be delivered in the framework of an essentially unchanging, and stable world. Athenian society was divided into three distinct groups: the philosopher kings, the auxiliaries and the workers. The first group were those who held political leadership and who had both control and power. Essentially they were supported by the auxiliaries. The workers were the rest of society. Athens was a strictly hierarchical society where neither social nor political change were encouraged, and where change was seen as contrary to good government. It was felt that the qualities of leadership were inherent and that men (in an essentially sexist society) were fitted through these qualities for an assigned role in society. Plato argued that ability was inherent and that the purpose of education was that men should be trained for these assigned roles.

This is a model that has had an enormous influence on the development of the school curriculum through many centuries in English education. In the immediate post-war period, for example, the whole concept of secondary education was essentially set in this model with appropriate education available for three different groups of children in society: the academic, the technical and the rest. Graham and Tytler (1993) have argued that the National Curriculum also strongly embraces this Platonist philosophy, through presenting a model of practice which requires that key knowledge is set in a generally academic framework, with an emphasis in testing through a generally memory-based format. For children with SEN, particularly those with poor memory skills and who learn most easily through practical applications this is a largely inappropriate model of practice. It is an approach which has led them to be unable to demonstrate their personal knowledge in an appropriate way; the result of which has been to encourage personal frustration and demotivation.

Encyclopaedeism
The encyclopaedic model of education emerged at the time of the French Revolution in 1789. It was based on the premise that the content of education should encompass all human knowledge. This was a reflection of a French society that was more egalitarian than that

prevalent in ancient Greece. In contrast to the Platonic ideas outlined above, it argued that all men were capable of reason and the
acquisition of moral ideas. Further, it reflected the view that, in this
respect at least, there was no sharp division between the ruler and the
ruled. In many respects its base was that personified by Descartes, 'I
think therefore I am'.

It is this philosophy that was established on the continent of
Europe as the standard approach for educational provision. As far as
children with SEN are concerned this is a more appropriate
approach. It is one that, theoretically at least, accommodates their
needs within its overall framework.

Pragmatism

The pragmatic model of the curriculum appeared in late nineteenth
century America and was based on vocational and problem solving
issues. Proponents of this approach argued that realistically it was
not possible to attempt to teach all knowledge. The body of this is far
too great and as such some selection of material has to take place.
Within this its key focus was on the development of methods of finding solutions to problems. These should be based on vocationally
useful topics, as well as adding to the individual pupils' general education.

In this context individual children and their personal needs are
paramount. It is their needs that should be the key to the curriculum
that is selected. This model has had considerable influence on recent
curriculum content until the introduction of the National
Curriculum. This can be exemplified in the primary school through
the influence of the Plowden Report (1967) on the management of
the curriculum. The influence of this model can be seen on curricula provision in the special school as well as that used with pupils with
SEN in mainstream schools (Brennan 1971, 1985, Westwood 1975,
1993).

The discovery method

The discovery model of the curriculum has been increasingly evident in the post-Second World War period. This approach, while
taking into account some of the features of the pragmatic model
described above, originated from the views of Socrates and particularly those of Rousseau (1762). This model, from the period of the
Plowden Report (1967) to the introduction of the National
Curriculum (1988), was particularly influential in primary schools.
During this period its influence was also felt increasingly in secondary education.

The discovery approach relies heavily on the concept of 'readiness' in children's learning and in developing their motivation, through their interests and experiences. It was a model which was commonly used with pupils with SEN, to take into account not only their readiness to undertake learning and their motivation but also the pace at which this could be done successfully. Although it was an approach which, as far as pupils with SEN were concerned, had much to recommend it, criticisms of its value were made in the second Black Paper on Education (1969). Increasing pressure from those parents who disliked the concept of readiness and sought a more interventionist approach from teachers, along with that from politicians in the 1970s and 1980s (detailed by Graham and Tytler 1993) led to the discovery method being largely discredited and its abandonment at the time of the introduction of the National Curriculum (1988).

AN HISTORICAL OVERVIEW

Curriculum development in England and Wales is a comparatively recent phenomenon, certainly compared with other aspects of education. Throughout much of this century it was not regarded as a necessary part of centralised planning by politicians of any major political party. This may account for the remarks of the Schools' Council (1971, p. 2) which saw it as 'ramshackle and disconnected'. Young (1971), with this in mind, argued that there was virtually no theoretical perspective or research on the curriculum that could explain how it persists and changes.

The first developments in this field began to appear only during the 1960s, through work by Schon (1971), Havelock (1971), Bennis, Benne and Chin (1969) and House (1974) in America and Stenhouse (1975) in Britain.

INFLUENCES

Before looking specifically at changes in the curriculum for pupils with SEN it is necessary to outline and discuss factors which are important in the whole field of curriculum development. This will help to place such developments into an appropriate context. It is not easy to determine why curriculum change was initiated only recently and was not a feature of educational development earlier in the century. One can only pinpoint various possible influences. One factor was related to the consequences of the Russian successes in space during the latter part of the 1950s. This initiated a reconsideration of school curricula, in the USA particularly, when the shock of being beaten in the space race had considerable impact. This also had a considerable impact on curriculum thinking on this side of the Atlantic.

Change in the approach to educational provision was another factor. The debates and discussions that developed in the post-war period on such topics as comprehensive schooling, mixed ability teaching and the development of courses in the aftermath of the raising of the school leaving age were important factors in initiating debate on the curriculum in the secondary school.

The introduction of new subject areas in schools was also important. New courses based around the new technologies had to find their place in the curriculum. Again this was accompanied by changes in the secondary school as part of the consequences of the raising of the school leaving age. Subjects such as environmental studies, humanities and social studies were taught to pupils in the upper secondary school and new approaches had to be found to do this. As a consequence, there was an influence on what was taught in the lower secondary school. Further, these changes in secondary schools can be linked to those which occurred in primary schools, particularly in relation to the influence of the Plowden Report (1967) and the recommendations that it made for the primary school curriculum.

For Young *et al* (1971) and Goodson (1988) there is a social construction element to the curriculum that must be taken into consideration. As part of this Goodson (1988) argued that one cannot hope to understand curriculum selection, without taking into account both its social construction and its historical context. In its widest context, taking into account the needs of all children, this is set in the context of four key criteria: the knowledge which has most worth, what should be taught, how it should be taught and to whom it should be taught.

The concept of worth is not regarded as merely an issue of personal choice, or even a whole school issue. It is far more a societal concern and decisions with respect to this reflect the commonly held values and traditions of a society in order to prepare its children for adulthood. This must also bear in mind the point made forcefully by Peddiwell (1939), Stenhouse (1975) and James (1968) among others, that society is a living and changing organism; and it must prepare its children to be able to adapt to the changes that will occur in their lifetime.

Tansley and Gulliford (1960) and more recently Brennan (1985) asserted that the selection of curriculum content for pupils with SEN should be based on a number of key features. For Tansley and Gulliford (1960) a model of great importance was what they described as the core and peripheral curriculum. The core curriculum they described as the essential information and knowledge that should be passed on to a child, as opposed to the more peripheral information which might be introduced later. They outlined three essential pillars of thinking about the curriculum. These, they argued, were the logical sequencing of material and the psychological and social needs of the child.

Brennan (1985) considered the design of the curriculum for pupils with SEN. He concentrated firstly on a hierarchical model of knowledge for children with SEN. This was based on a three tier concept of what a child *must* know to participate in society, what they *should* have knowledge of and thirdly what it would be useful if they *could* know. These were further described in terms of the relationship between mastery and familiarity, understanding and awareness. In practical terms, he argued, these levels will be determined, for those with SEN, in relation to the expectation and experience of the teacher on the one hand and the level of ability and skill of the individual pupil on the other.

THE INFLUENCE OF WARNOCK

The Warnock Report (1978) continued to add to knowledge about appropriate curricular programmes for children with SEN. It addressed a number of significant issues. These included access to the curriculum and the tone in which it was taught as well as selection and classroom management issues. The report regarded the curriculum for pupils with SEN not only as a series of highly relevant theoretical points, but also, in practical terms, similarly to Tansley and Gulliford (1960) and Brennan (1985). The report analysed the curriculum in terms of its purpose, the process by which it was selected and how it was modified. Its purpose for pupils with SEN was set out in terms of awareness of moral values, imaginative understanding and a capacity for enjoyment. The report also detailed other important curriculum considerations for children with SEN. These included its accessibility for all pupils and the tone in which it was taught.

ACCESS

Accessibility, the Warnock Report (DES 1978) recommended, must take into account the availability of appropriate equipment and facilities for pupils with SEN to successfully undertake the tasks that they are set. This was set in the context of resourcing such needs which the report recommended would need to take into account any modifications that needed to be made to school buildings to fully accommodate pupils with physical impairments and specialised teaching aids to allow full access to the curriculum for pupils with particular disabilities.

The Warnock Report argued that a key aspect of curriculum provision for children with SEN in mainstream schools was the degree to which it had been modified to meet their needs. This modification was defined in two ways: in terms of the material presented to pupils and the objectives which staff set for individual pupils in order to give them access to the whole curricular range.

Curriculum access for pupils with SEN was also described in the report in terms of differentiating the management of their learning. The Warnock Report supported the view that the curriculum for pupils with SEN should be strongly influenced by the level of work of which children were capable and the pace of delivery with which they could cope. This, it indicated, should be supported by appropriate learning material. The impression gained by the committee was that although there was generally great concern shown by staff in mainstream schools for individual pupils, the curricular provision which was offered was often unsatisfactory. It was found to be limited in scope and insufficiently challenging, as well as showing inconsistencies between schools.

SELECTION

Difficulties in the delivery of a differentiated curriculum have been acknowledged by both the National Curriculum Council (NCC 1989) and professional organisations such as the National Association for Remedial Education (NARE) (1990). The NARE report outlined the key issues particularly well. These included the range of ability to be found in the normal classroom situation, varying rates of maturation, levels of personal motivation and the personal expectations of pupils, differing learning styles and variations in previous pupil experience. The report also re-stated the need for continued vigilance over the development of positive attitudes by teachers, the development of a good classroom climate and the importance of a strong partnership between teachers, their pupils and parents. Further, this report indicated the need for developing individual curriculum planning, extra in-class support and special classroom arrangements for certain pupils.

Barthorpe and Vissar (1991) described the essential aspects of differentiation as: the content of the lesson in relation to the ability of the children, the approach in relation to the level at which it is taught, the pace at which it is delivered, the way in which it is assessed and recorded.

TONE

The issue of tone referred to in the Warnock Report related to the school as a working environment and the effect that this might have on pupils with SEN. This the Warnock Committee, along with others such as Hargreaves (1967), Willis (1977), Haigh (1977) and Hinson and Hughes (1982), among many others, identified as a critical factor in the personal development of many children, not exclusively those with special needs.

By promoting the concept of one set of general curricular aims for all pupils, the committee considered that this would help to lessen the distinctions which it had observed between the curricular and organisational provision made between remedial and other teaching groups in the mainstream school. It argued, through the concept of the continuum of special educational needs, that this division could no longer be made.

This was a point made also in the research conducted by Hargreaves (1967), Willis (1977) and Hemming (1980), all of whom indicated that if adequate arrangements were not made for all pupils, some would exhibit secondary motivational and behavioural difficulties through a growing frustration with the school system.

MANAGEMENT

The Warnock Committee argued that one way forward was a form of support from other teachers for pupils with SEN in mainstream schools. This was seen by both the Warnock Committee and NARE (1978) as a role for the special education department or the Special educational needs co-ordinator (SENCO). At the time of its publication there was little evidence of the successful application of such practice in schools, although examples of developments in this area were discussed by Rogers (1973) and Watts (1978).

In calling for change the Warnock Report (1978) acknowledged the lack of available information on good curriculum practice and it called not only for schools to pay attention to the issue, but also for both research and extra funding to finance developments in this area.

SURVEYS OF DEVELOPMENTS

Despite these innovations, which gathered pace as a result of the influence of the Warnock Report, the evidence of contemporary surveys conducted during the 1970s indicated a wide range of variations in practice for children with SEN. Brennan (1979) described many departments responsible for pupils with SEN as weak, and Westwood (1975) similarly described the organisation of the timetable as fragmented to the point of incomprehensibility. Cameron (1981), in drawing these points together, argued for the need for better planning and organisation. He made particularly unfavourable comparisons between the situation in schools and those in industry and business.

During the 1980s there were indications of some developments taking place. A nationally based programme to aid curriculum development for pupils with SEN was initiated in some secondary schools in various parts of the country. The Low Attaining Pupils Programme (LAPP), was set up by the DES (1982) to aid the development of curriculum provision for the least capable 40 per cent of pupils in secondary schools. Harland and Welton (1987) described this programme as innovatory in a number of ways, not only because of its approach to the task but also because it was the first major initiative to be managed directly by the DES.

Positive responses were also reported in development of approaches in individual curriculum areas. Hinson and Hughes (1982), despite some criticisms, reported overall positive developments. The literature of the period provides indications of an explosion of activities in the major curriculum areas. These included the teaching of reading (Moyle 1982, Dobbin 1985) and spelling (Cripps 1979, Jones 1980, Peters 1985). This has spread to individual subject areas such as geography (McKenzie 1981), maths (Blane and Englehardt 1983, Whayman 1985), biology (Watkins and Lewis 1983) and history (Wilson 1985). Material was also being produced to give advice on adapting material (Harrison 1980, Hartley 1972) and the implementation of individualised learning programmes (Davies 1978).

However, more radical changes were being demanded. Hegarty and Pocklington (1982) called for fundamental changes to the curriculum for pupils with SEN. Jones (1983) pointed out that the very nature of the management of change in schools meant that this was unlikely to happen and that the best that could be expected was evolutionary developments. Nevertheless both she and Clunies-Ross and Wilmhurst (1983) were optimistic. Their evidence, supported by that of HMI (1988), indicated that nearly every secondary school made some form of provision for pupils with SEN. This was a much better figure than that produced by HMI (1968) some 20 years earlier.

TOWARDS A NATIONAL CURRICULUM

Discussions over curriculum selection and particularly that of Britain's declining economic and political influence in the world have led to considerable debate during the last 50 years as to the most apposite approach to curriculum selection and planning for all pupils. Increasingly, since the end of the 1970s, there has been a greater involvement by governments in the direction this has taken. Guidelines issued by the DES (1979, 1980, 1985) and the Assessment and Performance Unit (APU 1981) are indications of this.

This activity led the DES (1981) to produce a definition of the school curriculum. It was argued that the curriculum comprised all the opportunities for learning provided by the school. This, they indicated, included the formal programme of lessons that were set out as eight, and later nine areas of experience. These areas of experience were based on many of the traditional school subjects, such as geography or science, as well as newer ones such as technology. Other areas of opportunity identified for pupils included extra-curricular and out-of-school activities. The culture fostered by the school in terms of its climate of relationships, attitudes and styles of behaviour were also identified as being important factors in aiding the development of learning for pupils. These opportunities, it had been argued by the DES (1979), were set in the competing demands exercised by parents and society at large.

The views expressed by the DES (1981) as to the direction of curriculum policy and the concept of areas of subject experience that should be available to all pupils was not universally accepted among those working with pupils with SEN. Hinson and Hughes (1982) argued that, for these pupils to be in a position to avail themselves of these areas of experience, there would be far-reaching implications for the provision that was needed. Hegarty and Pocklington (1982) were similarly critical, regarding the eight areas of experience as being too tight a framework. Further, they commented that for such pupils the concept of the curriculum must be set as a loose description of activities. Moseley (1977) argued that even limited objectives were beyond the capabilities of certain children.

Surveys by Clunies-Ross and Wilmhurst (1983), Stakes (1990) and HMI (1986), and criticisms by The School's Council (1981, 1983), HMI (1985) and the DES 1981) indicated that the range of subjects offered to pupils with SEN in the first three years of secondary school was often restricted, either by design or through guiding pupils away from certain subject areas. The subjects most likely not to be offered to those with SEN were foreign languages, science and history and geography. From this evidence it was increasingly claimed that the range of learning opportunities for pupils with SEN was restricted by individual schools' practices.

THE NATIONAL CURRICULUM

Difficulties with the overall organisation and control of the curriculum detailed above, combined with tensions over the purposes of education, particularly from the business community, and certain political influences, led to an increasing degree of central control over the curriculum. The 1988 Education Act took much of the responsibility for the choice of curriculum away from schools and the individual teacher and centralised it through the National Curriculum programme. The development of the National Curriculum, along with the introduction of the Code of Practice (1994) and OFSTED inspections (1993) has had a major impact on curriculum organisation and delivery for children with SEN throughout their years of compulsory schooling.

The National Curriculum was described by Moon (1994, p. 1) as 'representing one of the most significant educational reforms of the century'. It heralded a major shift in national educational policy, a shift which was controversial. The Parliamentary Bill was introduced after a consultation period which resulted in the largest response ever to any legislative proposals. These responses, collected by Haviland (1988), indicated that an appreciable number of people were strongly critical of the proposals.

The Act was seen as fundamental to the changes needed to the development of educational thinking and management. Thatcher (1993) viewed it as helping to redress the influence of the ideas of more left-wing teachers. Baker (1993), the Minister of Education, saw it as changing the focus of educational provision, to one which was producer dominated. He regarded it as necessary to encourage competition, choice and freedom in education: all of which he considered were vital for the development of excellence in schools. It is arguable that these factors were of considerably less relevance to those pupils with SEN.

The National Curriculum programme was set in four key stages of pupil development, corresponding to the process of compulsory schooling, with two stages at both primary and secondary levels. The compulsory curriculum was divided into core and foundation subjects. The core subjects were: maths, English, science and Welsh (in Wales), while the foundation subjects were: history, geography, technology, music, art, PE and at Key Stages 3 and 4 in the secondary school, a modern foreign language. The teaching of RE that was made compulsory in 1944 was continued without it being classified as either a core or foundation subject.

Each of these subjects was set in a framework of attainment targets, programmes of study and assessment stages. The attainment targets were defined as the knowledge, skills and understanding which children were expected to have at the end of each key stage. The programmes of study were related to the knowledge, skills and processes required to be taught to each pupil. The assessment stages referred to the arrangements that were put in place to assess pupils at the end of each key stage. These assessments were to include examinations and tests.

As far as pupils with SEN were concerned, the thrust of the legislation created a dilemma between their inclusion in the National Curriculum programme and the need for integrated provision. It was argued that the national curriculum arrangements would have a divisive effect on pupils with SEN and their parents. Both the NARE and the Rathbone Society (Haviland 1988) were concerned about the effects of attainment tests on pupils with SEN. NARE was also concerned about the effect of the performance of pupils with SEN in schools in the increasingly market-orientated approach detailed in the Act. It was also thought that pupils with SEN would depress the level of achievement in schools and therefore not be welcome in mainstream schools.

At the outset of the debate there was a considerable lobby from teachers and professional organisations for the inclusion of pupils with SEN in national curriculum arrangements. Without this, it was felt, the concept of integrated education would be severely damaged. The parliamentary debates, particularly in the House of Lords, were furious. The influence of Lady Warnock in particular was strong and eventually, through a series of amendments, the concept of an inclusive programme for all was carried. These are reflected in the National Curriculum Council (NCC) documentation, particularly Circular 5 (1989), which emphasised the importance of all children participating in the attainment targets and programmes of study. *A Curriculum for All* (NCC 1989, p. 1) set this participation in the context of a 'broad and balanced Curriculum including the national curriculum', while a further document *The Whole School Curriculum* (1989) set out the opportunities for such children in the light of these developments.

Leonard (1988) argued that the suitability of the programme of work had to consider three groups of pupils: those with statements, those with statements pending and those unlikely ever to get a statement. Regarding those with statements he pointed out the clear need for them to be written to indicate how far the requirements of the National Curriculum could in reality apply for each child. Beyond this he indicated the need to preserve as much flexibility as possible and to use broad descriptions. Those without a statement he described as being in a 'grey' area. He argued, in the light of these arrangements, that on the surface at least provision appeared to be 'adequate enough' (p. 38).

The arrangements as set out in the Act allowed for possible flexibility for some pupils. Where it was considered necessary, pupils with SEN were allowed to be disapplied from the programme or for it to be modified for two periods of up to six months throughout their compulsory schooling. In such circumstances the head teacher of the school had certain duties. The head must inform the parents of the decision and also indicate what alternative provision had been made. If they were unhappy with this situation parents had a right of appeal. In the first place this was to the head teacher, and then latterly, if their doubts remain, to the governing body of the school. Leonard (1988) argued that such a move was expected to affect only a small proportion of pupils and that the overriding philosophy was positive. He did however admit that, at that stage, it was difficult to see just how this arrangement would work in practice.

Review of the arrangements for those with SEN was undertaken by the NCC (1993), HMI (1990, 1991) and Dearing (1993, 1996). These reports provided positive information as to the overall thrust of the National Curriculum for pupils with SEN in mainstream schools. The most frequently cited benefits from these reports were: the provision of a broader curricular programme with better overall coherence, the raising of teacher expectations, a clearer structure within which the differentiation of teaching material could be undertaken, the improvement in assessment procedures and better record-keeping by teachers.

An NCC (1993) survey was similarly positive, indicating that teachers of pupils with SEN strongly supported the entitlement of all pupils to the broad and balanced curricular programme. These teachers also indicated their lack of enthusiasm for the disapplication of pupils, asking for a more positive approach to it. Further, they felt the need for proactive developments to identify and share examples of good practice and the need to develop a broader system of assessment to recognise pupil achievement when the standard tasks are inappropriate. Further positive points that emerged related to the writing of statements (which it was indicated should illustrate positive ways of accessing the National Curriculum) and guidance on the differentiation of material and teaching across the whole ability range.

Nevertheless, a number of key issues relating to National Curriculum practice continue to cause difficulties. HMI (1990, 1991), despite their positive comments reported above, indicated that there continue to be difficulties in many schools. Teachers, both collectively through their unions and individually in the media, have indicated their doubt. Overall, the National Curriculum arrangements have been described in generally very negative terms by practitioners, in both its concept and practice. In this respect Stretton and Stott (1996) argued that teachers felt that they had lost a certain degree of their professional autonomy. Criticisms were widespread, not just from teachers working with pupils with SEN. Eventually these brought widespread changes to both its content and its assessment procedures. This occurred throughout the period from 1988 to 1993, and culminated with the changes of the Dearing Report (1993). Currently criticisms are being 'put on ice', as there is a five-year moratorium on any further changes.

As far as those with SEN were concerned, criticisms have been many and varied. Weedon (1994, p. 142) described the whole exercise as 'unhelpful and potentially damaging', while Riddell and Brown (1994) indicated that the overall view expressed by most in the field (including Swann 1992 and Weddell 1988) was hostile and perceived as particularly damaging to children. White (1991) and Stakes and Hornby (1996) went even further, suggesting that the National Curriculum is fundamentally irrelevant to many pupils, particularly for those who have need of a more socially-focused educational programme.

Difficulties can be identified from this literature. These include the lack of realism between the age-related key stages and the level of performance of certain pupils. This was a concern to many teachers, particularly when a child needed to work at a level below that of their normal key stage. This issue, critics argued, is compounded by the lack of time available to work with individual pupils in certain subject areas because of other priorities in the programme. Examples of this included the time needed to undertake and reinforce extra basic reading and maths work with those pupils who need it.

At secondary school level the National Curriculum for pupils with SEN was criticised for reverting to a watered-down academic style programme so condemned by Brennan (1979). Currently this includes a diet of Shakespeare and the classic authors. In this respect the key pillars of curriculum selection of breadth, balance and relevance outlined as key features in the 1988 Act, are questionable for pupils with SEN.

Other criticisms that have been raised are wide-ranging. These included Thomas (1995) who considered that the academic nature of the programme had led to a loss of sight of the pastoral and pedagogical work necessary with pupils. Allen (1994) argued that the pace necessary to work through the attainment targets militated against the smaller steps of progression needed and the necessary reinforcement of work for some. Further, she reported that because of the inflexible nature of some of the attainment targets, teachers of children with special needs were having difficulty in meeting the necessary requirements.

Supporting this view, Simpson (1993) argued, firstly, that the National Curriculum was not the most appropriate instrument for effective individual learning and, secondly, that although the overall concept was of entitlement the real issue was with regard to what pupils with SEN are entitled and to its value. Sweetman (1992) suggested that by its overall thrust towards the successful pupil, human nature being what it is, the National Curriculum was bound to create failures as it was focused essentially on the academic minority of children. This was a point supported by Graham and Tytler (1993) when he indicated that the key influences in its initiation were Whitehall and the representatives from the public schools.

The views of teachers about the National Curriculum have been reported in generally negative terms. There is continuing and overwhelming evidence both individually, through letters to the press, and through professional organisations, that the National Curriculum programme has pressurised them. Teachers have expressed a number of concerns. These include: a general lack of personal commitment to the programme, difficulties with its bureaucracy and a lack of confidence in the validity of the results of the SATs conducted at the end of each key stage.

Others, however, have been more encouraging: Lewis (1991) argued that the inclusive curriculum programme would aid the integration of children with learning difficulties into the mainstream primary school. Hegarty (1989) and Russell (1990) felt that it would encourage teachers to consider the progress of all pupils and provide for the active involvement of parents through their access to greater information. O'Hanlon (1994a) argued that the development of the inclusive curriculum would help to raise the status of both pupils and teachers, make their voices increasingly heard and act as a change agent for a greater degree of reflective practice. These points were accepted and underscored in the NCC guidance (1989) which also accepted the call from teachers to develop a national network to identify and share examples of good practice of planning, organisation and the development of provision throughout the country.

These issues must be taken together with others which have emerged as a consequence of the 1988 Education Act. The statementing procedure is now more complex and schools find making satisfactory provision in small classes more expensive. The pace of the teaching and sometimes the level of expectation has led to pupils with SEN not always being able to absorb all the information they are offered. By finishing work more slowly they are sometimes not completing the tasks required. Further as a consequence of this they are likely to remain confused, frustrated and even disaffected by their experiences.

In this context the view of Leonard (1988) is most apposite. He argued that a society's priorities for the education service can be judged by the manner in which the service provides for pupils who have come to their schools at a disadvantage. Using this test, Leonard (1988) states the 1988 Act has failed. With this in mind he proposes that the responsibility for this lies not with society but with the Government whom he suggests has 'little regard to what society really needs in its public education service'.

OTHER ISSUES

The effect of the National Curriculum has been only one of a number of recent important curricular issues affecting pupils with SEN. One of these is the question of resources and another relates to the role of the teacher in the decision-making process.

Curriculum resource priorities are currently determined through factors which are not always relevant to children with SEN. These can, on occasions, be largely political decisions. For example, money spent on the SATs process for them is largely wasted. Further, the repeated reductions in annual budgets allocated to schools continue to squeeze resources. As a consequence there is a constant threat of increases in overall class sizes and cuts in teaching staff. The effects of this are less contact time for those pupils with SEN and a consequent growth in frustration among staff at not being able to perform their work in a professionally satisfactory manner.

The financial constraints imposed since the introduction of Local Management of Schools (LMS) in 1988 have had a severe impact on initiatives directed towards children with SEN. One example of this was the Reading Recovery scheme which was introduced and financed by a government initiative announced at the time of the 1992 general election. This scheme, so successful in New Zealand, was heralded as a possible major development for younger children with weaknesses with literacy skills. Despite this central government finance the scheme has recently been withdrawn only part-way through several projects which are evaluating its effectiveness. The motives for such a decision have to be questioned, not only in terms of the possible educational reasons, but also at the economic and political levels.

Recent changes have been made largely without reference to the teaching profession. Uniquely in the recent history of curriculum innovation in this country, there has been no attempt to seek consensus between the various strands of teacher opinion, the government and civil service. The government and the teachers have, in the years since the 1988 Education Reform Act, seemingly worked to a different agenda. Such a situation cannot be to the benefit of anyone, let alone those children who have the greatest learning difficulties. In practical terms, the influence of thinking on the National Curriculum which has been identified and discussed above in taking into account only the interests and abilities of a minority of pupils, and largely excluding the needs of some 20 per cent of the weakest ones, cannot but create disharmony and tensions. This, in the longer term, can only detract from what must be the main focus of the education system: the development of the abilities and skills of all pupils.

CONCLUSIONS

The history of curriculum provision for pupils with SEN has been fraught with difficulties. In part this has been a perceptual difficulty within society which has associated physical and mental weakness. It can also be related to difficulties in selecting an appropriate curriculum model for these pupils. The concept of a watered down academic curriculum, based on the Platonic model, dominated particularly in secondary schools for many years. For the less academically successful this was an inappropriate approach.

These problems have been compounded by the way in which the work and progress of pupils with SEN has been assessed. The current focus of examinations in mainstream schools concentrates on the assessment of skills which children with SEN have difficulty in acquiring, by means of inappropriate techniques. Neither the SATs at the end of each key stage of the National Curriculum nor GCSE examinations (in their present form) are helpful to indicating the learning achievements of pupils with SEN. It is important that appropriate curriculum provision is made for all pupils, however, the evidence indicates that for up to 20 per cent of pupils much remains to be done.

Integration: the eternal dilemma

INTRODUCTION

This chapter will focus on the integration of pupils with SEN into mainstream schools which has been debated throughout the period of compulsory education. This debate has been one of the most problematic associated with special educational provision.

The discussion will take into account three areas of change. Firstly, philosophical and moral issues, as well as societal expectations for children with SEN will be considered. Secondly, we will consider the changes in methods used to identify children with SEN and the practical and organisational issues of importance. Thirdly, changes that have occurred as a result of the pressures brought about by interest groups directly involved in the field will be looked at. These groups include teachers, parents of the children with SEN and the children themselves, as well as those indirectly involved such as politicians and other professional groups.

Comparisons will also be made between thinking on the integration of pupils with special needs in this country and others throughout the world.

THE CONCEPT OF INTEGRATION

Cole (1989) argued that the concept of integration of children with SEN is not static but has been subject to changes in both fashion and interpretation throughout the century. This can be seen through changing attitudes in society brought about by the enhancement of medical and psychological knowledge, the political and financial commitments that have been made and by the decisions about provisions for SEN made by individual schools and LEAs.

As pointed out in Chapter Two, for much of this century society has had no consistent policy regarding people with SEN, either while they are at school or afterwards. Further, for much of this time there has been no consistent planning. Often other factors have had a crucial influence on developments. As a consequence of this, forms of integration into the mainstream have developed by accident rather than design. This has often been based on the influence of interested individuals. The decisions taken have sometimes been unilateral and confined to individual LEAs or even particular schools. This has led to different levels of integration for pupils with special needs in different parts of the country.

Cole (1989) also pointed out that the evidence relating to patterns of change with regard to integration is complex and contradictory. This can be seen in the Victorian and Edwardian periods, where although there was a reduction of boarding provision for children with SEN this was accompanied by extensive development of systematic separate day school provision. This complex situation continued throughout much of the century.

The concept of 2 per cent of children with special educational needs receiving their education outside mainstream schools is long-standing. The basis for this figure originated from the work of Burt (1935) and Schonell (1941) and was reinforced by the official figures released by the DES (1964) and then the views of the Warnock Committee (DES 1978).

However, the evidence indicates that there are considerable variations on this figure. Swann (1988) estimated that, at its peak in 1983, the special school population in the UK was only 1.54 per cent of the total school population. DES statistics indicated that estimates of the special school population in the preceding years varied considerably. The proportions ranged from 0.81 per cent in 1957 to 1.44 per cent in 1987. Comments from the DES/Audit Commission report (1993) suggested that this number has again been reduced in recent years.

What is without dispute is that there are considerable variations in the proportions of pupils in special schools in different parts of the UK, with wide variations between LEAs. The reasons for this are varied and relate to decisions taken by individual LEAs. Factors which have contributed to these decisions include: the amount of special school provision that is available in the area, the selection procedures that are used and the prevailing attitudes towards integration in both the LEA administration and local mainstream schools.

From the beginning of compulsory schooling the key debate in special education has mainly, but not exclusively, centred on the issue of the most appropriate form of provision for pupils identified as having SEN. Throughout the period of mass education a number of issues have been highlighted as central to this debate. Among the most important of these are discussions of the most effective way of educating these pupils to best meet their needs and those of the wider society. Another key issue relates to the values and benefits of having such children with their peers in mainstream schools as opposed to being educated in separate institutions.

ORIGINS

The debate as to how best to provide for the education of children with special educational needs is closely linked to changes in the attitudes in the wider society towards such children which have been discussed in Chapter Four. It is a debate that has taxed teachers and the parents of these children as well as school administrators throughout the twentieth century.

It might be expected that the debate on integration in the UK was initiated at the time of the introduction of compulsory schooling in 1880. Certainly, it was argued by Lawson and Silver (1973) that the history of special education began seriously in the 1890s, with Acts of Parliament making provision for various groups of pupils with difficulties such as blindness, deafness, the physical defects and epilepsy. The introduction of compulsory education however served only to highlight the issues. The evidence indicates that debates over the education of these children pre-date this move by many years. Pritchard (1963), Sutherland (1981), Hurt (1988) and Cole (1989) traced these back to the latter part of the eighteenth century. For a number of years around the turn of the nineteenth century, little more than experimental forms of provision for children with SEN had been established. These often focused on those with particular and clearly obvious physical difficulties. Hearing, sight and speech problems were the most common. Where provision was made it was often not only separate but also conspicuously pernicious. This was the case both in regard to the language used to describe the schools (an asylum (*sic*) for the deaf was opened in London in 1792 and one for the 'indigent' blind in Liverpool in 1793) and in terms of the ambivalence with regard to the best approach to be used to meet their needs.

The provision available was often dependent on the individual philosophy, whims and financial constraints imposed by pioneers in the field. The evidence collected by Pritchard (1963), Cole (1989) and Lloyd and Gambetsi (1991) shows that throughout the major part of the nineteenth century this was haphazard to say the least. In some parts of the country, children with SEN received their education within a framework of integrated provision within the mainstream school, while in other areas children with similar difficulties were being educated in separate special schools.

THE INTRODUCTION OF COMPULSORY EDUCATION

The introduction of compulsory education brought its own problems for the integration of children with SEN. This brought into the equation not only those with clearly discernible physical handicaps but also those with learning and social difficulties. At a time when both the salaries of the staff and the money available to schools was determined by the children's ability to pass the annual examination of the inspectors, this was a key area of difficulty and friction.

There is however conflicting evidence on this point. Tomlinson (1982) and Ford (1982) indicated that the system of payment by results was an issue, and that until this was dropped in 1890 it was a concern that as many children as possible with learning difficulties were excluded from classes so that the full payment was made. In turn, she argues, this led to the demand for the exclusion of such children. Similarly she argued that there were calls for the exclusion of disruptive children from the mainstream school. Mainstream school teachers supported this policy in order to concentrate their efforts and skills on the rest of the class.

Hegarty (1987) argued similarly, that the introduction of compulsory education served to increase the pressure from teachers for provision to be made for those children who failed to learn successfully. There was scant provision for this throughout the country and adequate provision proved difficult to organise. Arnold (1883), an HMI inspector of the time, noted numerous complaints from teachers on his visits to schools that many pupils were prevented, by the nature of their intelligence, from reaching the standards required by the Revised Code (1862). Similar comments can be seen in individual school log books of the period.

Cole (1990), however, largely dismisses this argument particularly the position taken by Tomlinson (1982) and Ford (1982), arguing that there was little evidence to indicate that the school system was sinking under the weight of handicapped pupils. In his view, the need for exclusions was largely based on guilt experienced by teachers, who felt that a special class or special school would allow for the provision of a more meaningful education than either they or their fellow teachers could provide.

Ironically, in many areas of the country there was no provision for either those in special classes or special schools and teachers had to rely on punishing children to produce social compliance, or where that failed condoning truancy or seeking expulsions. In the circumstances engendered by the Revised Code there was little incentive for staff to take on the work involved in teaching such pupils.

THE EGERTON COMMITTEE

The Egerton Committee was the first formal attempt to investigate and report specifically to Parliament on the needs of children with disabilities. The placement of such children within the education system was one of the issues which they had to address. In the event its recommendations did little to help quieten the debate over the integration of pupils with SEN. Two diametrically opposed views can be identified in the evidence presented to the Commission. There were those who considered that the deaf could best be educated in separate institutions and those who saw integration as the best approach. The evidence presented by the former group was largely based on observations of social contact between pupils who were integrated into elementary schools and the rest of their peer group. In contrast, the integrationalists generally based their opinions on more philosophical views about the overall desirability of integration for this group of pupils. They argued that this would benefit both the children themselves and the wider society.

Pritchard (1963) and Cole (1989) cited evidence from head teachers who had observed a lack of social contact between children who were deaf and their peers in the playground, despite the encouragement of the teaching staff, for this to take place. The evidence collected by the Egerton Committee provided some of the reasons for this. These included the view that deaf children saw themselves as separate while others described this in mutually exclusive terms. One headmaster described a lack of any 'visible desire on the part of the hearing to associate with the deaf' and a similar 'lack of eagerness' on behalf of the deaf.

For those who saw integration as desirable there were four main factors of importance. These were factors that have set the tone of the debate for many years since. These related to: the need to avoid a distortion of the views of those who were deaf due to living in closed communities: the need to avoid the institutionalisation of children that occurs in such circumstances; the Christian perspective of the need for the strong in society to assist the weak and the need to take into account the choice of the parents of these children.

THE SHARPE COMMITTEE

Through the recommendations of the Sharpe Committee (1898) the cause of integration took a backward step. Much of the evidence collected from teachers and other professionals with regard to this debate was contradictory and inconclusive. Observations by the members of the Committee led them to believe that much good work was being done with segregated pupils. Particular emphasis was made by the committee that these pupils were not being teased and harassed by their peers in mainstream schools. It was this as much as anything else which led them to recommend separate special schools for such children, rather than integrated provision or special classes in mainstream schools.

THE INTER-WAR PERIOD

The debate on integration did not dissipate following the Royal Commission. Tomlinson (1982) pointed out that the influence of the Eugenics movement (discussed in Chapter Four) was at its height in the 1920s and their view clouded many of the judgements which were taken. The evidence collected by the Wood Report (1929) and the inconsistencies in its recommendations are one example of this.

The Spens Report (1938) which was so influential in secondary school provision in the post-war period came down strongly on the side of the segregationists. The report called for the streaming of classes in secondary schools in order to help those pupils who needed special provision. However, it can be argued that this at least acknowledged the expectation that some pupils in the mainstream secondary school would need some form of extra provision and that schools would be expected to provide this. Further, this recommendation also underlined, at least in part, the fact that large numbers of this group of pupils were already integrated locationally, and to some extent perhaps socially, within the mainstream school system.

The Spens Report (1938) along with that of the London County Council (1937) and Schonell (1937) reinforced the 'one group' philosophy of provision, underlining the view that as many pupils with SEN as possible should be integrated into mainstream schools. Nevertheless, there were those who continued to doubt it. The Board of Education (1937) in a pamphlet on pupils with learning difficulties, argued that such an approach would produce 'sink classes' and would undermine the self-confidence of pupils placed in them. It was not clear if they thought that separate schools could be regarded as 'sink schools'.

The practice of segregating weaker pupils for special attention was one that had been used to some effect in other countries as well as Britain during the inter-war years. This was particularly the case in the United States. Inskeep (1930), a keen supporter of this approach, explained the policy for this as being one that could prevent children with SEN from floundering along in the regular grade class. A similar view was taken on this by Ingram (1932) and in this country by Burt (1931) and Kennedy Fraser (1932).

THE POST-WAR PERIOD

The attitudes displayed in Parliament during the passage of the 1944 Education Act gave some indication of the change of views regarding pupils with SEN in society at the time. There was an indication of growing tolerance and understanding of children with difficulties and the philosophy of the Act reflected this. This was reflected in the recommendations it made. The Act called for as many of the pupils who had been ascertained in the categories detailed for children needing special educational help to be educated in mainstream schools.

However, it has been argued that this philosophy was not fulfilled in practice. The Warnock Report (1978) cited two main reasons for this. These were made in the light of some 30 years of experience of working with this Act and in the light of considerable pressure from certain quarters to integrate all pupils as fully as possible within mainstream schools.

Firstly, the Warnock Report argued that the statutory framework of the 1944 Act was not conducive to the concept of special educational treatment or to its development in mainstream schools. The Act proved to be dichotomous by requiring that those children with severe disabilities (particularly physical or mental disabilities) were to be educated in special schools, while those with what was regarded as less serious problems were to be educated in mainstream schools.

Secondly, it argued that the practical considerations of the post-war world impeded the development of provision for special education throughout the country until at least the mid-1950s. Factors that contributed to this situation in the immediate post-war period included the scarcity of building materials, a rapidly rising school population (which further dispersed precious resources), the building regulations (which provided standard size classrooms for 30 pupils in the secondary school, a number too large to encourage the development of SEN provision). Further, there was a shortage of specially trained teachers and other professionals required to undertake the assessment and education of such pupils.

Nevertheless, the influence of the 1944 Act on the integration debate cannot be underestimated. The DES (1964) described it as not only reflecting changes in outlook but also far sighted by its provisions. The Act embodied a completely new attitude to children with disabilities. Primarily they were recognised as having special needs. Further, it also required that the categorisation of pupils who should receive help was to be based on solely educational grounds.

Integration continued to be a key issue from the time of the 1944 Act. Pressure for a change to a greater integration of pupils from special schools into mainstream schools built up during the 1950s and 1960s. In many respects, despite the importance of the 1944 Act and its considerable influence, in reality it solved nothing. The delineation of the categories, initially regarded as so important, served only to exacerbate the situation. It was a cause of considerable frustration for parents, pupils and their teachers, particularly those working in separate special schools.

Barton and Tomlinson (1984) linked these issues to complex social, economic and political factors that can be identified in an historical analysis of the period. They argued that these can be related to the frustrations of the wider society and the attitudes of parents to the educational system as a whole. They also argued that these factors need to be considered in relation to the experiences of the professionals working in the education system as well as the identifiable concerns that were present relating to the needs of individual children.

Hegarty and Pocklington (1981) and Fish (1985) although acknowledging the complexity of the circumstances, argued that the impetus towards greater integration of pupils with SEN was based on clearly identifiable factors. In their view, these included: improved assessment techniques during this period, a growing concern for human rights, the status of minority groups, reports of practice from other European countries and innovative developments in the UK. The importance of the last two points was however minimised by Gallagher (1974), who observed that little of the theory of integration was based on scholarly research, but more on relevant social issues in society.

Evidence of the strength of opinions for the greater integration of children with SEN can be ascertained from the literature of the early 1970s. Rowe (1972) provided some indication of the growth of positive views about integration among teachers and parents alike, while Woodward (1972) supported this from the point of view of teachers.

The views of disabled people themselves were most clearly demonstrated in the Snowdon Working Party (1979) which indicated an overwhelming dislike of segregated schooling.

The DES (1974) demonstrated their awareness of the situation by arguing that contemporary opinion was increasingly in favour of the integration into mainstream schools of children who were usually placed in special schools. Further it added (incorrectly according to its own statistics (DES 1975)) that such developments were already taking place more than was commonly realised.

Rowe (1972) perhaps reflected the reality of the situation more closely. She argued that it would be some time before even the mildly handicapped would be supported satisfactorily in mainstream schools. Nevertheless, evidence from Pumphrey (1972) and Tuckey (1972) indicated that the opportunity for change was growing in an educational climate where it was seen that both philosophically and socially there were benefits for pupils with considerable difficulties who were integrated into mainstream schools.

The literature of the period between the setting up of the Warnock Report in 1972 and its publication in 1978 demonstrated increasingly that there was an increasing pressure for integration. Accounts from various parts of the UK by Garnett (1976), Roberts and Williams (1980) and May-Wilson and Broadhead (1979) described such developments.

However, despite the evidence of initiatives towards the greater integration of pupils into mainstream schools and indications of a more positive climate to encourage this, statistical evidence from official reports such as Schools Council surveys (1968, 1970, 1971), the Bullock Report (1975) and HMI (1979) showed that the national picture was very patchy, and the great majority of secondary schools were in no position to accommodate these pupils. Further, where attempts had been made to provide integration schemes, there was little evidence of any analysis of the development of good practice or of formal evaluations of its effectiveness.

As far as the practicalities of integration were concerned, reports at the end of the 1960s tended to suggest that for those pupils with SEN who attended mainstream schools the situation was highly unsatisfactory.

A School's Council survey (1968) indicated that at that time only one out of three secondary schools made any formal provision for those pupils with SEN whom they had on register, let alone seeking to accommodate more. The research completed as part of the Bullock Report (1975) found that although two thirds of schools regularly or occasionally withdrew pupils for special help with reading, only one third had special classes or remedial departments. A similarly depressing picture of the organisation to accommodate the need of pupils was provided through the School's Council surveys of 1970 and 1971.

An HMI (1979) survey of secondary school practice overall showed that in the intervening years nothing had changed. It was similarly unambiguous in its findings on this point. HMI (1979) found that specialist teaching time for pupils with difficulties decreased each school year during their secondary education, and by years ten and eleven it had virtually disappeared. They indicated further that the curricular programme on offer lacked coherence and differed widely from that offered to their more able peers.

The criticism of the curricular programme was swingeing. HMI (1979) indicated that it gave little real choice, was of poor quality and lacked any real sense of enquiry, stimulus or appeal to the imagination. Certain subjects were not offered to pupils with SEN at all. Despite this the pupils did have certain advantages. These generally included small teaching groups and a smaller number of staff teaching them. HMI (1979) considered that one contributory problem was the lack of experience of staff working with these pupils. Their enquiries indicated that some 12 per cent of staff in this area of the school were in their probationary year, while some 35 per cent had fewer than five years experience.

The survey also indicated that staff had low expectations of children with SEN. This, they indicated, was an important contributory factor to the poor self-image and low expectations displayed by pupils who had been observed. This pessimistic survey stated there was a lack of experience within schools to carry out the appropriate diagnosing, resourcing and management of pupils with SEN.

PRESSURES

In the light of the depressing findings outlined above, it is hardly surprising that calls were being made for an overall review of provision. By the early 1970s these calls were coming from all directions, from individuals and official bodies representing both educational and political interests as well as parents themselves.

The Guild of Teachers of Backward Children (1972) gave its reasons for this as being in order to counter a reluctance to acknowledge the extent and gravity of the problems posed by disadvantaged pupils in schools. Support was also forthcoming from the Head Teachers' Association (1972), which described the problems of organising and structuring help as 'immense'. At the same time there were calls from politicians of all persuasions to support the setting up of a formal enquiry to investigate the circumstances, and to make recommendations as to the future shape of provision for all children with SEN.

THE WARNOCK REPORT

The committee set up under the Chairmanship of Lady Warnock was the Government's reply to these calls. Central to its recommendations was the overall integration of as many pupils with SEN as was viable into the mainstream school. The Warnock Committee felt that a more proactive stance was now necessary. The 1970 Act had brought all children, even those with the severest disabilities, into the education service. The Education Act (1976) required LEAs to provide for the education of all pupils with SEN in mainstream schools in preference to special schools. This was the case unless it was impracticable, incompatible with the efficient running of the school, or involved unreasonable public expenditure.

The Warnock Report (1978) has been described by Bushell (1979) as having a vital effect on provision for SEN. The Report regarded the issue of the integration of pupils into the mainstream school as the greatest contemporary issue of SEN. The Committee considered as many pupils as possible should be integrated into the mainstream school system. The Report argued that this was a fundamental right in relation to both the opportunities available to this group of pupils and also in relation to their personal self-fulfilment. The integration of pupils with SEN into the mainstream school alongside their peers was seen as part of their preparation for adulthood in the wider society.

Although somewhat controversial, even radical, from the schools' point of view, this was not an entirely new concept. Certainly in relation to adults, the Thomas Report (1961) and the Snowdon Report (1976) had argued the need for this. These reports also pointed out that there be no difference between the aims of education for the disabled and those for the rest of society.

The Warnock Report (1978) set the number of pupils with SEN into a wider context than had previously been publicly accepted. It argued that approximately one in six children (18 per cent) have long-term SEN and that one in five children would need special educational help at some point in their school career. Therefore, 20 per cent of children attending school was regarded as the proportion of children needing special help at some time during their schooling. This figure was in line with estimates from previous reports and was well above the 2 per cent of pupils who were educated outside the mainstream school. The figure of 20 per cent also acknowledged that the vast majority of pupils with SEN were already receiving their education within the normal provision of ordinary schools.

Beyond the question of whom the Report defined as its focus, it also defined different levels of integration that had been observed in schools. The findings indicated that there were three levels, which were not discrete but overlapping. These levels were described as a hierarchical progression of greater integration. These were categorised as locational, social and functional integration.

The Report outlined locational integration as existing where special classes or units were set up in the mainstream school and shared the same site. This level of integration was an indication of geographical location rather than any form of contact that might have existed. The survey conducted on behalf of the Committee indicated that in some cases that were observed, special classes or units were effectively separated from the rest of the school in all respects and there was little or no organised contact between them. It was for this reason that this level of integration was described as 'the most tenuous form of integration'.

Social integration was defined as where pupils attending a special class or unit, although taught separately for much of the time, were able to interact with their contemporaries from the mainstream school. In some cases the Committee observed pupils sharing organised out-of-classroom activities with each other.

Functional integration, the report indicated, was achieved when the locational and social associations of all children led to joint participation in educational and social programmes. This, the Committee argued, was the purist form of integration. In the most ideal of circumstances children joined their peers on either a part-time or on a full-time basis in normal timetabled classes and were able to make a full contribution to the activities of the school.

It was pointed out that functional integration made the greatest demands on the mainstream school. This was the case because of the need for careful planning for both class and individual teaching, to ensure that all pupils benefited whether or not they had SEN. Further, the Committee suggested that not only was this form of integration uppermost in the minds of most people when the issue was discussed but also that it was the ideal form that should set the standards for schools to strive towards.

INTEGRATION AFTER WARNOCK

It is important to remember that it was the 1976 Education which encouraged the integration of children with SEN into mainstream schools. This legislation appeared two years before the publication of the Warnock Report, suggesting that the decision to encourage increased integration came, not from the careful deliberations of the Warnock Committee, but from the DES. In fact, the Committee effectively side-stepped the debate regarding the advantages and disadvantages of integration and simply re-affirmed the requirements of the 1976 Act. These were that, subject to certain criteria, pupils with SEN were to be educated in ordinary schools in preference to special schools. The four criteria were: that integration was in accordance with parental wishes, that the child's educational needs could be met, that it would be consistent with the efficient use of resources and that it would not detract from the education of other children.

However, despite the clear stipulation of these criteria in the 1981 Education Act, many LEAs in England subsequently developed special education policies which involved progression towards a situation in which all children with SEN would be integrated into their local schools (e.g. Humberside County Council 1988). Such policies have also been adopted in New Zealand (Chapman 1988), Scotland (Henderson 1991) and in some parts of North America (Shaw 1990).

In a programme broadcast on national television in 1987, Mary Warnock stated that such a policy would be more expensive to implement than existing arrangements, particularly in the transitional phases. She noted, however, that LEAs were intending to make these changes within existing levels of resources. Further, she pointed out that, if such integration was to occur without the provision of adequate resources, then children with SEN would be worse off than if they remained in the segregated facilities which were scheduled for closure. In fact, in a television programme broadcast in January 1992, she stated that, although the 1981 Act encouraged schools to integrate children with SEN, 'it was recognised that there would always be a need for special schools.'

DEVELOPMENTS IN THE THEORY OF INTEGRATION

Notwithstanding the above comments, the literature on 'inclusion', or a policy of integration of children with SEN into ordinary schools, has been growing rapidly in the last few years. Some examples will now be discussed in order to illustrate the developments in this theory.

In the USA, Gartner and Lipsky (1989) proposed an alternative to the continuum of provisions, from segregated to special schools, through special classes to mainstream schools which has been a widely accepted model for the delivery of special education services for many years (Deno 1970). They suggested that, instead of the severity of the SEN determining the degree of segregation necessary, it would determine the amount and range of services provided to children who would all be integrated into mainstream schools. That is, children with mild SEN would receive a low level of resourcing, those with moderate SEN a higher level and those with severe SEN the highest level of support and resources in their integrated setting.

Another theoretical development is the suggestion that the techniques of co-operative learning (Johnson and Johnson 1987) can be used in order to effectively educate children with SEN in mainstream classrooms (e.g. Self *et al* 1991). Guidelines have been provided in order for teachers to establish classrooms in which every aspect of organisation and instruction is intended to create an environment in which individual differences are respected and children help each other to succeed (Stainback and Stainback 1990).

Stainback and Stainback (1990) have also been instrumental in promoting the concept of support networks as necessary components of effective integration. They have provided guidelines for programmes of staff development and for the development of strategies necessary for supporting children with SEN in mainstream classrooms.

A major innovation in the USA has been the development of the Adaptive Learning Environment Model (ALEM). This is a model which embodies effective teaching practices in order to facilitate successful integration of children with special needs into mainstream schools. The components of the ALEM include: support services delivered by special educators in mainstream classes, curriculum based assessment, highly prescriptive teaching, individual education plans, self management of learning experiences and flexibility in arranging learning environments (Wang and Wallberg 1983).

The most far reaching theoretical developments to emerge from the field of special education in the USA in recent years is the Regular Education Initiative (REI) (Lloyd, Singh and Repp 1991, Wang, Reynolds and Wallberg, 1988). The basis of the REI is the proposal that mainstream schools should assume responsibility for the education of all children, including those with SEN. There would then be no need for a separate special education system, since the expertise and resources required for children with SEN would be delivered from within ordinary schools.

In the UK much of the recent literature on integration has focused on guidelines for developing whole-school policy and procedures for meeting SEN (Dean 1989, Hegarty 1987). That is, writers have spelled out the roles and tasks which teachers need to fulfil and the attitudes, skills and knowledge which they require to do this successfully. For example, procedures for identifying children with special needs are discussed, as are the arrangements for supporting these children in mainstream classes. Such developments are also professional development issues and the roles of teachers working with children with SEN is further explored in Chapter Seven in this book.

Another emphasis in the UK literature has been the organisation of 'support teaching' (Booth, Potts and Swann 1987, Garnett 1988). This reflects a change in the role of special educators, in implementing integration, from working directly with children with SEN to supporting other teachers with such children in their classes. A further recent suggestion by Dyson (1990) akin to the development of REI in the USA, is that SENCOs in mainstream schools should be 'effective learning consultants'. Such consultants would be responsible for analysing and planning learning and managing resources in order to help teachers cater effectively for individual differences among pupils within their classes. The skill and knowledge used by such consultants would be mostly those needed for special needs work. However, their focus would not be specifically on children with SEN but on facilitating effective learning throughout the school.

Clearly, there has been recent progress in the elaboration and dissemination of the theoretical basis for effective integration. However, this theory appears to have gone further towards integration of the whole pupil population with SEN than was apparently intended by the legislation. The theoretical approaches to accommodating the effects of this and some of the research evidence regarding the effectiveness of integration have taken this into account. At the same time the indication of the resources which have been made available and the practical considerations for the classroom teacher seem not to have moved along at anything like the same pace.

RESEARCH ON INTEGRATION

The publications on integration projects in the UK (Hegarty, Pocklington and Lucas 1982 and Jones 1990) have been mainly attempts to describe good practice, rather than to evaluate the effectiveness of this integration for the children with SEN who were involved. The few accounts which have included some form of evaluation have reported both positive and negative outcomes for the children involved (e.g. Beasley and Upton 1989). However, several reviews of the literature on the effectiveness of integration were published in the 1980s. These have dealt mainly with the integration of children with moderate learning difficulties since this has been the group on which the majority of research has focused.

In the earliest review Gottlieb (1981) addressed the four main reasons proposed by Dunn (1968) in his influential paper, as to why special classes for children with moderate learning difficulties were not justified. These, he argued, were because for pupils with moderate learning difficulties: achievement is greater in regular classes, there is less stigmatisation of them there, special classes increase racial segregation and there is greater individualisation of the curriculum in ordinary classes.

Gottlieb, however, drew different conclusions. As far as pupil achievement is concerned he concluded that there was no clear difference between segregated and integrated provision. He was similarly sceptical on some aspects of social adjustment for pupils with SEN. Further, he argued that pupils who were integrated into mainstream schools were more stigmatised and rejected by non-handicapped peers than their segregated peers. As far as he could see the data available suggested that mainstreaming practices were not rectifying the racial imbalance in classrooms. Finally, he also reported studies which found a low level of individualised teaching in both special and ordinary classes.

Madden and Slaven (1983) in their review focused on academic and social outcomes as compared with segregated placements. Most studies reviewed were considered methodologically flawed or demonstrated no significant differences. An analysis of the few methodologically adequate studies suggested that integration was more effective than special class placement. This was particularly the case when mainstream teachers were trained special educators who individualised the instruction they provided.

However, Zigler and Hodapp (1986) found from their review that children with moderate learning difficulties did equally well on academic achievement in segregated and integrated settings. Further, while integrated children exhibited higher levels of social skill, they were routinely stigmatised by their non-handicapped peers. Levels of racial segregation were found to be about equal in the two types of setting. Integrated placements were found to cost less than segregated ones but there was less individualisation of programmes than in segregated placements.

Chapman (1988) found that children who had been integrated had lower levels of self esteem than children who were segregated. Danby and Cullen (1988) in reviewing the evidence for five educational assumptions inherent on the policy of integration found no support for the assumptions that educational efficacy, social benefits and reduced stigma would result for children with learning difficulties who had been integrated. Regarding the assumptions of improved parent involvement and the effects on non-handicapped peers they found that so little research had been done it was not possible to comment.

Beyond this Lindsay (1989) considered the findings of previous reviews on educational achievement, social interaction and stigmatisation and concluded that support for integration on empirical grounds was lacking. Fuchs and Fuchs (1988) also concluded that there was a lack of research evidence for the success of the ALEM approach described above.

A summary of the evidence gathered to date indicates that the reviews conducted have generally failed to find support for the effectiveness of integration in attaining the goals espoused in this rationale. Apart from the lower cost of integrated placements, the reviews have found little evidence that the goals of integration are being met. Thus it appears that greater educational attainment, increased social skills, reduced stigma, increased self esteem, greater racial integration, improved parental involvement and the individualisation of instruction does not necessarily result from integrating children with moderate learning difficulties into mainstream classrooms.

TRENDS

A recent study by Swann (1991) has reported a trend towards increased integration of children with SEN into ordinary schools. This study found that between 1982 and 1990 the numbers of children with SEN segregated into special schools decrease in 44 LEAs and in 15 of these the decrease was greater than 25 per cent. On the other hand, levels of segregation increased in 15 LEAs and in three of these the increase was greater than 25 per cent.

A study of integration practices in eight countries conducted by Pijl and Meijer (1989) found that the proportion of children with SEN aged six to 17, who were not functionally integrated varied from 1.5 per cent to 4.2 per cent. In this survey England and Italy had the lowest levels of segregation while Belgium (3.5 per cent), the USA (3.8 per cent), Holland (3.9 per cent and West Germany (4.2 per cent) had the highest levels. Sweden (at 2 per cent) and Denmark (2.4 per cent) had levels of integration in the middle range.

The overall findings of the study indicated that in each of the countries at least 1.5 per cent of children were not functionally integrated. That this is the case, even in Italy, where in principle special and regular education have been fully integrated for all children since 1977, suggests that as a policy the integration of children with SEN is a goal which is very difficult to achieve in practice.

CONCLUSIONS

In conclusion, although there have been considerable developments in the theory of providing integrated education to pupils with SEN and there is a clearly identifiable wish from many parents and teachers for this, it seems that current policies have gone well beyond the intentions of the legislation which initiated them. Further, there has been a lack of research evidence to support the effectiveness of integration for children with SEN in ordinary schools.

It therefore appears that currently held views on integration have evolved mainly from policy decisions, theoretical developments and examples of best practice in some schools rather than the implementation of the intentions of existing legislation or research evidence regarding its effectiveness.

The Code of Practice (DfE 1994) takes a moderate stance on the integration issue by emphasising the importance of having a continuum of SEN provision to meet a continuum of needs while making the point that the needs of most children with SEN can be met within mainstream schools. Some writers (e.g. Booth 1994) have openly criticised the Code for recognising the need for a continuum of SEN provision rather than adopting a philosophy of inclusive education, which aims for the maximum integration of children with SEN into mainstream schools and classes. However, inclusive education is currently regarded to be a controversial approach, partly because of a growing tide of criticism from special educators in North America such as Lloyd, Singh and Repp (1991) and Kauffman and Hallahan (1995) and partially because of the lack of research evidence supporting the effectiveness of inclusive approaches in mainstream schools (Hornby 1992, Lingard 1994).

Finally, it needs to be emphasised that many of the current changes in the practice of education in the UK, particularly as a consequence of the 1988 Education Act, are working against the interests of many children with SEN who are integrated into mainstream schools. Fish and Evans (1995) have suggested that:

> The current education policy, rooted in economic competition and personal choice is not sympathetic to social integration and as a

result, the integration of disabled children, young people and adults into school and society receives less priority. A re-appraisal of the concept of integration and an analysis of the economics of minority choices is now necessary. (p. 100)

Recently Lingard (1996) has criticised the proposition espoused by those such as Dyson and Ainscow supporting the inclusive philosophy on the basis that it is both idealistic and impractical. Lingard considers that by promoting these philosophical models of integration, these writers, along with other leading academics in the field of special education in the UK, have distracted attention away from other possible innovations designed to improve the effectiveness of education for children with SEN. This supports our contention that the lack of agreement as to the extent to which pupils with SEN should be integrated into mainstream schools has retarded progress in the development of provision for them.

Professional development and training

INTRODUCTION

The professional development of teachers in the area of SEN has been an increasingly important aspect of work undertaken at initial training and post-qualification levels. Such professional development has been an important agent in assisting changes in both classroom practice with children with SEN and in developing the wider role of specialist teachers throughout mainstream schools.

Throughout the early period of compulsory education instances of development were largely incidental and heavily dependent on the influence of individual teachers working with pupils with SEN. It is only in the last 30 years that teacher training for SEN has been subject to more organised planning.

This chapter will focus on changes relating to the professional development of teachers of pupils with SEN. It will concentrate on a number of key aspects. These include the development of courses for those interested in working with children with SEN at both initial training and in-service levels. These developments cannot be considered in isolation, therefore account will be taken of the changing role of teachers working in this area. The participation of professional associations in the increasingly widening role of teachers working with children with SEN across the whole school will also be detailed. Finally, the development of competence-based courses, which are likely to predominate in the immediate future, will be discussed.

FIRST DEVELOPMENTS

As has been detailed in earlier chapters, provision for children with SEN difficulties in mainstream schools did not receive much attention until the end of the eighteenth century. Initially, provision was often started by individuals interested in working with children with hearing and sight difficulties. There is evidence, from Britain, the rest of Europe and in the USA of individuals helping to teach disabled children the rudiments of the three 'Rs', often in small groups.

Increasing knowledge about techniques for teaching children with various disabilities gathered pace only slowly at first. Its dissemination was haphazard and hampered by superstition and poor communication. It was only in the late nineteenth century that medical science and the development of disciplines such as psychology began to supersede the superstition and fear which dominated attitudes towards disability.

Progress was further hampered by personal prejudices surrounding the development of certain specialist techniques. Acceptance of these sometimes had to wait until there were other developments in medical and educational research. The work of Louis Braille is one example of this. His work with the blind was ignored in Britain for over 50 years. Similar circumstances pertained in the debate over teaching methods for the deaf.

Often during the eighteenth and nineteenth centuries schools were set up by benefactors and individuals who sometimes took account of developments made elsewhere but often based teaching approaches on ideas of their own. In these circumstances they would often train staff themselves and pass on teaching techniques in this way. The value of some techniques and approaches used was however questionable. The Committee on Defective and Epileptic Children (1897) reported that some children in this group learned as much from each other as they did from their teachers. The overall evidence indicated that although many children with SEN were being taught to read and write and do arithmetic, the teaching was often of a poor standard and left them with little understanding.

THE ADVENT OF COMPULSORY EDUCATION

The introduction of compulsory education in the latter part of the nineteenth century had not been accompanied by any real awareness of either the nature of pupils' learning difficulties nor how they could be best alleviated. School log books of the time and comments from HMI, as well as anecdotal evidence from the literature of the period, are indicators of the difficulties experienced by many elementary school teachers. Despite these difficulties, there was no provision for the training of teachers as part of the 1870 or 1880 Education Acts.

Pritchard (1963) and Cole (1989) indicated that, in schools for the teaching of the blind and the deaf, founders of schools would typically provide some training for their staff. However, in mainstream schools there was little if any provision of training for helping children with SEN. Pupil teaching had a largely 'sitting with Nelly' philosophy and lecturers working in the normal training schools had little to offer in the area of techniques for teaching pupils with SEN. In the nineteenth century the practice of teacher training was counter-productive to such developments. Contemporary practice indicated that there were approved ways of teaching and the focus in training was on drilling teachers to use these approaches in their classroom practice. These approaches may have been satisfactory for the majority of children in the elementary school but there is considerable anecdotal evidence from the fiction of Bennett, Lawrence and Dickens that it was inappropriate for all. The Cross Commission (1888) was very critical of this approach, asserting that teachers were being drilled in merely mechanical processes.

The importance of the need for change in the professional development of teachers was recognised as early as 1893 when the Charity Organisation Society advocated the need to improve teachers' skills. Pritchard (1963) and Tomlinson (1982) summarised the educational experience of pupils with SEN at the end of the last century as one where there was a lack of good teachers and good teaching. These factors led to difficulties in recruiting good staff.

Recruiting the better teachers to work with pupils with SEN was difficult. It was considered that one way of encouraging good teachers to do so was to pay them more than their colleagues. This was the policy in London as early as the end of the nineteenth century, where the School Boards introduced a policy of appointing good certificated teachers to their special schools and paying them extra money. Pritchard (1963) indicated that at one such school, opened in 1895, the Board paid the qualified staff who worked there £15 per annum more than those who were working in elementary schools.

The level of qualifications of those who worked with children with SEN has been another major issue which has had to be addressed. At the end of the nineteenth century children with SEN in mainstream schools were taught by uncertificated staff and pupil teachers. In this sense it can be seen that those pupils with the greatest learning difficulties were often taught by the least qualified and most inexperienced staff. To some extent this argument has persisted throughout the period. (A similar, contemporary parallel can perhaps be drawn with the use of teachers aides who have no teaching qualifications working with pupils with statements of SEN).

Evidence from Blishen (1955), Taylor (1963) and Partridge (1966) indicates that new recruits, in their first teaching post, often started their career with a timetable excessively biased towards the academically weakest pupils. On many occasions teachers were expected to teach very large numbers of pupils. Contemporary evidence indicates that in some schools at the end of the nineteenth century the typical class size could be as large as 70 pupils. Those pupils with difficulties were often collectively placed in Standard 1, as their progress had not warranted promotion, or in Standard 0 where such an arrangement had been made. In this respect some evidence presented to the Sharpe Committee (1898) argued that class size for such pupils should be set at no more than 20. Beyond this it was advocated that all head teachers and most classroom assistants in special schools should be certificated teachers and no one under the age of 21 should be employed to teach there.

Concern was also expressed as to the effects on the health of teachers who worked with children with difficulties. The Sharpe Committee (1898) raised serious misgivings about the appointment of staff in special schools on long term contracts. It was suggested that, on health grounds, no contract for teachers working in special schools should initially be longer than five years. However, it was argued that those who wished to continue after that time should not be prevented from doing so. This theme was also taken up by HMI at the time, one of whom wrote of it not being safe to keep a woman at this work continuously and without a break for a year. The emphasis on female teachers was an indication of the gender balance of those working in elementary schools.

However, little was done to address these issues and changes were slow in coming. Some 50 years after these calls were made the Ministry of Education (1954) was still pointing out that teachers in special schools needed breaks from their duties there. This document suggested that teachers in special schools should spend periods of one year at a time in mainstream schools. It was felt that this would avoid teachers in special schools lowering their standards and expectations of pupils over a period of time.

The Newsom Report (1963) produced similar arguments for those teachers who spent much of their time with pupils with SEN in mainstream schools. Here, however, the reasoning was based on the need for teachers to keep in touch with the realities of the whole school. It was thought they would not become so isolated and perhaps somewhat confined by the intellectual and social restrictions of their normal daily work.

The developments in teacher training during the first half of this century certainly saw changes in the areas of qualifications and remuneration. Teachers working in special schools generally gained qualifications, although some were employed as unqualified teachers until the mid-1970s. By this time qualified staff in special schools were also paid an extra allowance for the work they did, over and above that paid to their mainstream school colleagues.

SPECIALIST COURSES

The issue of specialist courses for teachers working with pupils with SEN, or wishing to develop skills in this area was not really properly addressed on a national scale until the early 1960s. In an attempt to develop the professional skills of teachers some university departments introduced specialist courses and work was undertaken in certain teacher training establishments to develop in-service training focusing on children with SEN.

The Newsom Report (1963) recommended the development of specialist courses, indicating the importance of developing knowledge and skills in this field. This was underlined politically by Chataway (1963), a junior minister at the Department of Education, who called for all places on such specialist courses to be filled. Nevertheless, provision of training for SEN remained haphazard. Bushell (1976) described the national pattern as hazy, while McNicholas (1976) argued that it was isolated from the rest of post-qualification courses. Guidelines issued by the National Association for Remedial Education (NARE) (1976) indicated that the problem was mainly locational, in that courses leading to advanced qualifications in special education were not available to some interested staff within 100 miles of where they lived. Professional organisations such as NARE attempted to address this issue by calling for greater liaison between the colleges and the LEA advisory services as well as working with distance learning organisations such as the College of Preceptors to develop award bearing correspondence courses.

Developments in training and the acquisition of appropriate qualifications were vital to avert continued problems of low status for teachers working in this field among their colleagues. Unfortunately, such moves remained low on the agenda of both local and central government. Therefore, despite calls from professional bodies and certain politicians, funding was difficult to obtain and campaigns to develop such courses produced limited results.

The findings of a survey conducted by the Warnock Committee indicated that primary school teachers felt inadequately trained to work effectively with pupils with learning difficulties. Later, studies by Croll and Moses (1985) and Clunies-Ross and Wilmhurst (1983) came to the same conclusions. These surveys only underlined the importance of continued professional development for teachers of children with SEN and similarly the need for an input on initial training courses.

INITIAL TEACHER TRAINING

The Advisory Committee on the Supply and Education of teachers (ACSET 1984) stated that specialist training in the area of SEN should not be provided until the completion of initial training. However, all initial teacher training (ITT) courses now have to contain an SEN component. This focuses on the knowledge required to undertake the duties detailed at Stage One in the Code of Practice (DfE 1994). Many institutions have responded to this by subsuming SEN matters into components of their courses, making them the responsibility of all tutors. Some ITT courses have organised free-standing, non-compulsory courses for their students but these are not currently widespread and are at the discretion of individual institutions. Nevertheless, ACSET, The Council for the Accreditation of Teacher Education (CATE) (1984) and the DES (1989) all indicated that, at this level, teachers should already have basic professional skills. These included being able to identify children with SEN, how to meet these needs and when and how to enlist specialist help.

Recent documentation, however, indicates that, despite an increased integration of children with more complex difficulties into mainstream schools, SEN education for ITT remains unsatisfactory. DES circular 24/89 (1989) indicated that the preparation students received on initial training courses was diverse and variable. Hegarty and Moses (1988) were similarly critical, arguing that at initial training level awareness-raising was not enough for new teachers to cope with the problems they were likely to find in the classroom. The Council for National Academic Awards (CNAA) (1991) pointed out that the extent to which SEN awareness raising activities were being undertaken at the initial training level was a matter of debate.

These points have been reinforced by Garner (1996) who argued that too many newly qualified teachers are totally unprepared for the challenges posed by pupils with SEN in mainstream school class-rooms. His research indicated that only one third of students under-taking ITT received six or more lectures on SEN topics and about one third received no more than two lectures. Of 14 key points iden-tified as important at ITT level, newly qualified teachers had covered less than 50 per cent. Further, he argued, there was no coherent pat-tern of what was covered. His survey suggested that the formal input on SEN on ITT courses remained something of a backwater. His findings also showed that many teachers in training pick up most of their information on SEN in their school based training and that often they lack confidence in the skills required at the outset of their first job. Finally, he reported that, during the first term of their first appointment, only 50 per cent of newly qualified teachers felt confident enough to deal with children with SEN.

THE POST-WARNOCK ERA

Following the Warnock Report (DES 1978) there were two training priorities for mainstream schools: the development of the role of the teacher concerned with pupils with SEN and that of the head of the SEN department. An HMI survey (*op cit* 1979) outlined many of the problems at the time of the Warnock Report. While acknowledging the difficulties of providing successfully for these pupils, it also indicated a lack of appropriate expertise in the teaching staff for diagnosing and dealing with many of the difficulties that they faced.

Professional bodies, including The National Association for Remedial Education (NARE) and The National Council for Special Education (NCSE), were not only aware of this situation but also called for teachers working in this area to be less passive and make more positive moves to help themselves and their pupils. There were calls for teachers to come out of the broom cupboard and for there to be less of an 'educational ambulance service' approach. That is, providing first aid and comfort to the weak and wounded, rather than delivering programmes of work that would aid development of their skills and talents. In their view, it was vital that staff should take a wider interest in, and have a greater influence on the decision-making process in their schools.

Historically, the focus for those teachers working with pupils with learning difficulties in the mainstream school concentrated almost exclusively on the development of vocabulary and reading skills. This area of work had often been their sole responsibility in the school. However, in more recent years an increasingly wider remit for specialist teachers of children with SEN has been identified. Gulliford (1976), for instance, identified an increasing need for teachers of children with SEN to act in a liaison role with other staff. Gains (1980), Widlake (1984) and Daniels (1984) called for specialist staff to adopt an interventionist policy within the school in order to support pupils and other staff. They also argued that the whole staff had a responsibility for pupils with special educational needs.

It has also been argued for a similar role to be encouraged with the parents of these children, to keep both parties informed of developments and to share experiences. For McNicholas (1976) and Daniels (1984) the role of the teacher of children with SEN, along with that of the LEA advisor, was pivotal as an agent for change in the school. This, McNicholas (1976) argued, was not only necessary from the pupils' point of view but also essential to the development of a whole school curriculum policy in departments where previously the influence of staff had been minimised.

Daniels (1984) similarly called for closer links with LEA support service and with feeder primary schools in order to develop better understanding of each other and also to facilitate the easy passage of information between them. He also argued for closer links between special needs departments and other departments, arguing they should no longer consider themselves as operating in isolation from the rest of the school. Rather, they should realise their role as members of a team working with all teachers in the school.

Programmes and Guidelines
As part of the developments outlined above a number of programmes and guidelines for developing the training for staff teaching children with SEN were beginning to emerge in the early 1980s. McCall (1980), Bushell (1979) and Sewell (1982), for example, called for a three-phase model of development for the head of SEN departments in mainstream secondary schools. This called for the identification of all pupils in the school with special needs, the management of a special resource base in the school and a system of key teachers in different departments as a point of contact for staff about pupils with special needs.

In many ways these approaches were too narrow and did not cover the full range of activities and responsibilities of the special needs staff. A wider perspective was taken by Gains and McNicholas (1979) and the NARE (1979). They called for the teachers involved in special education to become more closely involved in the decision-making process regarding SEN at the highest levels in the school.

NARE (1980) detailed the key roles of the teachers of special education as: the assessment of pupils, the preparation and implementation of individualised programmes for pupils, a teaching and therapeutic role, a support role with other colleagues and a liaison role with other professionals and the parents of children with SEN. Dyson and Gains (1995) analysed the role of the SENCO in an attempt to identify the skills needed, while Lacey (1995) and Pickup (1995) provided practical advice which they considered were necessary to successfully undertake such work in schools. Similar analyses have also been completed at different stages in the educational system by Cocker (1995) (for infant schools), Harvey (1995) (for primary schools) and Bradley and Roaf (1995) (for secondary schools).

Despite attempts to improve the situation there are criticisms. Reid *et al* (1980) and Patrick *et al* (1980) pointed out that in-service provision to acclimatise teachers to the new philosophy continued to be at best 'patchy'. The economic climate and the shortage of resources meant that teachers continued to be inadequately prepared for working with this group of children.

In-service provision
In-service provision has been a commonly used approach for developing the knowledge and understanding of teachers about SEN and to promote changes in practice in schools. INSET has been used extensively since the 1981 Education Act. Often this has been accompanied by 'cascade' models of dissemination. This approach expects one member of staff who has attended such courses to share information with other staff in schools. Such an approach is a relatively inexpensive way for LEAs to pass on information to schools and as such has been used increasingly at times of financial stringency. However, its overall value is questionable as the messages received by colleagues are heavily reliant on the reporting skills of the messenger.

Gains (1984) pointed out that the availability of in-service provision for all teachers who need it had been slow to develop. Clunies-Ross and Wilmhurst (1983) and Stakes (1990) reported a considerable interest in this area. The survey by Clunies-Ross and Wilmhurst (1983) found that some 50 per cent of SEN staff questioned had attended at least one in-service course in the five years up to 1980. Two thirds of these had been concerned with elements of special educational provision. A survey by Stakes (1990) in the late 1980s showed that some 77 per cent of the schools questioned had at least one member of staff with formal qualifications in the area of special educational needs. These figures are a clear indication of the interest of staff and the time they had spent on personal development.

A support role
In the context of the Warnock Report, McNicholas (1984) and Daniels (1984) argued that teachers of pupils with special educational needs should act as catalysts for change within their schools. They envisaged an active role for SEN specialists in passing on their knowledge and skills to the rest of the staff. For many SEN staff this was a totally new venture. It was one which Lerner (1976) argued would place staff in a position in which they had very little background or experience. Nevertheless Stakes (1990) found that some

50 per cent of secondary schools had either initiated training provided by their SEN specialist or were at least thinking of doing so. His survey indicated that in the vast number of cases the initial incentive for this had come from the staff in the schools rather than through outside influences. Where these courses had been organised, the SEN staff responsible for them in 72 per cent of cases had felt confident enough to invite all the staff in the school to participate.

One possible spin-off from this sort of venture was a greater degree of whole-school co-operation and greater access for specialist staff into the classrooms of colleagues to work *in situ* with pupils with special needs. This development also allowed for discussions about the most appropriate learning strategies for children with SEN. Hinson (1985) argued that support was a way of reaching departments that remedial (*sic*) education could not reach.

The importance of a support role was discussed by NARE (1990) which indicated that the teacher providing this had a four-part role to fulfil. These were: advising colleagues on grouping and setting procedures for the target group of pupils, the development of ideas and techniques for all pupils with special needs, looking after a range of material and apparatus available to help teach pupils, and remedial work across the curriculum. Through the adoption of these roles it was hoped to encourage the development of specialist SEN staff working alongside the specialist subject counterparts.

As with the development of school-based courses, developments in the support teachers' role was commonly initiated by individual schools. Fish (1984) called for more staff to become involved in such programmes. However, Lavers *et al* (1986), Dyer (1988) and Davis and Davis (1988) indicated that developments in this area were slow and in many cases dependent on the initiative of individual staff.

The need for a co-operative role has emerged during the past few years, with the developing use of classroom assistants to help pupils with special educational needs. For the teacher responsible for co-ordinating this, particularly in the secondary school where a large number of teaching staff may be involved, there is a continuing need to develop inter-personal skills. Similarly, there is a need for the development of appropriate in-service and award-bearing courses to develop the skills of classroom assistants.

Fergueson and Adams (1982), commenting on these developments, pointed out that for good working relationships to develop a number of issues needed to be resolved. These included the development of mutual trust and the acceptance of intervention by the special needs teacher in the curricular programme offered by the subject specialist. Another issue is finding ways of marrying more closely the child-centred approach necessary for many pupils to learn with the organisational and curricular demands made in the normal classroom situation.

Experimentation
The post-Warnock era was a time of considerable experimentation for staff involved in teaching pupils with SEN and as such had an effect on the development of training. A variety of forms of provision were adopted in order to try to find suitable approaches for teaching pupils with SEN. Often these were undertaken in individual schools and the form they took was dependent on the views of the staff involved in consultation with the head teacher.

Developments which have been identified included a thrust towards a more 'team teaching' approach described by Fergueson and Adams (1982). The development of a more consultative role for specialist staff was indicated by Smith (1985) and strongly supported by Dyson (1990). The use of support teachers in mixed ability groups was discussed by Phinn (1983), Clunies-Ross (1984), Bowie and Robertson (1985) and Lewis (1984). The benefits of withdrawing pupils from other classes or situations was argued by Kelly (1981). The need to develop the role of the teacher of special needs throughout the whole school, in whatever situation they were needed, was described by Butt (1986), Hegarty *et al* (1982), Jones and Southgate (1983) and Giles and Dunlop (1986).

In an attempt to analyse the situation, McCall (1980) described those three most common forms of provision as the withdrawal system, the special class and the mixed ability class. Hegarty and Pocklington (1982) acknowledged that different forms of provision in different schools were inevitable and this should be expected.

Increasingly after the 1981 Education Act there was a proliferation of award-bearing qualifications for teachers working with pupils with SEN. Because of the changing role of the SEN specialist, professional development was seen as increasingly important for teachers working in mainstream schools with children with SEN.

These developments can be attributed to three key factors. Firstly, the number of pupils with SEN in mainstream education has increased as a consequence of the policy of increased integration. Because of this, all teachers need a greater understanding of both the disabilities of pupils with SEN and their educational implications.

Secondly, the increasing influence of government legislation on all aspects of working with SEN in schools has increased the need for information and for a forum for discussion in order to aid the development of good practice. Examples of this legislation include the development of the National Curriculum (1988), the introduction of both OFSTED inspections (1993) and the Code of Practice (1994).

Thirdly, the role of teachers of pupils with SEN has undergone considerable change, particularly during the past 20 years when increasingly those working with pupils with SEN in mainstream schools have adopted a wider cross-curricular role in schools, working in many subject areas with other staff. This has led to them adopting a greater advisory role with other colleagues. This has led to an increased need for knowledge about a range of appropriate strategies to adopt with pupils with SEN.

Developments in this area have provided their own tensions. As indicated in Chapter Three, resources have not always been readily available to meet the needs of teachers wishing to undergo further training and this has had financial management implications. Increasingly, in the period of Local Management of Schools (LMS) and tighter financial controls, the burden for this has rested with individual schools.

PROFESSIONAL DEVELOPMENT COURSES

There are essentially three types of professional development courses: those run as part of the INSET programme in the school or the local authority, those which are award-bearing and organised through higher education departments and those which are a combination of both these. Clunies-Ross and Wilmhurst (1983), HMI (1984), the NAS/UWT (1986) and Hegarty (1987) argued that all three of these approaches were important to the development of professional skills and changing practice with regard to SEN in schools. They asserted that each in their own way has an important role to fulfil and can act as an aid to teachers, not only in developing their knowledge and skills, but also in gaining recognition for it. Courses supporting the professional development of teachers working with pupils with SEN have taken all three forms in recent years.

Both Clunies-Ross and Wilmhurst (1983) and Stakes (1990) reported a willingness on behalf of teachers to undergo in-service training on SEN. Clunies-Ross and Wilmhurst (1983) found that some 80 per cent of staff indicated the importance of specialist training in working with children with SEN. Significantly, some 70 per cent of head teachers questioned in the same survey indicated that having formal qualifications was an important criterion in considering staff for SEN posts.

Hegarty (1987) and Nash (1993) saw professional development courses helping to generate school reform. Norwich and Clowne

(1985) described an approach that not only linked higher education institutes and LEAs but also was based on action research in schools. This approach, it was suggested, would not only give ownership to such projects but would also ensure that the one-term secondments it involved could be used to aid an agenda for change in participating schools. Other examples of close working partnerships between higher education and LEAs were described by Robson and Wright (1989) and Dust (1988). The benefits of such an approach were discussed by Sebba and Robson (1988) and Hornby (1990).

Hegarty (1987) argued that developments in individual schools would be helped if all teachers could recognise their responsibilities for all children and be committed to meeting their needs without undue recourse to external agencies. Earlier, Hegarty (1981) indicated that the benign attitude, so often shown to children with SEN, had never been appropriate. In his view, in-service work would help to develop the knowledge and skills of all staff in schools. Those teachers working with pupils with SEN were considered particularly important as it was they who had the relevant knowledge, experience and skills. In Hegarty's view they had the responsibility to share these with colleagues.

The reasons for the development of school-based INSET are very strong. The programmes which are undertaken are run by school staff for school staff and focus particularly on change in individual schools. Pupils with special needs will always benefit from wider dissemination of information strategies and techniques to help them. Indeed, staff responsible for SEN may also benefit in terms of their status and respect within the school. Further, in times of financial stringency where money to send teachers on courses is disappearing rapidly, this may be the only recourse for the school. However, there are dangers in this approach. Thomas (1993) argued that such a home-grown approach to professional development was incestuous and could lead to the recycling of bad practice. Essentially, he argued that teachers needed to draw on the experience of those from outside their own school.

The need for award-bearing courses on SEN has not diminished in the last few years, only the opportunity to obtain a place on one. In the early post-Warnock period both Clunies-Ross (1984a) and Cole (1989) reported that specialist courses flourished. Evidence from Clunies-Ross (1983a, 1983b) and Stakes (1990) showed that many more staff were able to participate, either through a term's or a year's secondment. Nevertheless, even then the difficult financial climate did not allow as many as might have benefited to participate.

One of the ways that was used extensively to provide staff with information on the details of the 1981 Act was the development of courses for SENCOs. These were often organised by individual LEAs. This approach allowed the LEA to focus on the implementation of policies in their particular area and also minimised costs.

This approach was part of a programme known as 'cascading' information into schools. During this period of considerable change in a wide range of areas relating to SEN provision, the member of staff with responsibilities for SEN would generally attend short courses, often of a day or half a day in duration. Part of their responsibilities would be to transmit the information they had received to other colleagues on their return to school. Using this approach, it was considered, would facilitate the transmission of key information effectively into schools.

The number of teachers seeking secondment for courses on SEN was highlighted by the requirements of the 1981 Act. The demand outstripped the number of full-time secondments available. This has not been helped by the gradual erosion of available secondments which has occurred since the mid-1980s. This situation has resulted in an increase in a new form of INSET based on a modular approach to awards, and generally undertaken by teachers on a part-time basis. The 1980s saw a proliferation of this trend as noted by several writers (Harnett 1986, Clench and Taylor 1986, Daniels, Porter and Sandow 1988, Robson, Sebba, Mittler and Davies 1988 and Dust 1988).

THE CURRENT SITUATION

Currently, professional development for teachers working with children with SEN continues to be a problem area. There is little finance available to support the secondment of teachers in large numbers, while the need for training for teachers in the area of SEN in mainstream schools has increased. In recent years the demand for in-service courses has far outstripped their supply. These problems are compounded by the increase in teacher workload. This has had a consequential effect on how they use their free time, when they may have considered undertaking professional development courses. As a consequence of recent changes, teachers now not only give up their free time after school to attend such courses but also increasingly pay their own fees. The issue of professional development is one which SENTC (1996) identified as being in need of urgent attention. The SENTC report argued that such developments are vital, so that teachers can meet the demands made upon them. It was also considered important that good professional development courses were available to all teachers. Firstly, it is important that not only those who are willing and can afford it are able to participate and secondly, so that all schools are in a position to avail themselves of the training provision that is available.

In recent years such courses have increasingly been arranged on a modular basis with a growing flexibility. These modules are generally directed towards particular topics. In this way, teachers can attend courses relevant to them and are able to build up credits towards award-bearing courses over a period of time. Development nationally in relation to the credit points allowed for these awards has also allowed for a greater degree of movement and flexibility between the awarding bodies. The introduction of the concept of the Accreditation of Prior Learning (APL) and, to some extent, the introduction of the Accreditation of Prior Experience and Learning (APEL) is likely to increase this.

FUTURE TRENDS

The development of mixed ability teaching and the integration of larger numbers of pupils with SEN into classes in mainstream schools has meant that the role of the class teacher in the education of children with SEN is increasingly important. Essentially, the Code of Practice (DfE 1994) has identified the tasks of the class teacher to include the teaching and learning of their pupils, classroom organisation and management and liaison with other professionals, parents and the community.

In the past century the identification of the skills required to undertake such tasks has been based on a variety of models. Our approach to training has not been based on any singularly prescriptive model, and in many respects it is not scientific. Teaching and classroom management skills have been developed by subjective factors and personal preferences, with competence judged subjectively by teachers' colleagues. The pupil teacher certainly started off with the 'watching Nellie' model and there is much to indicate from the writing by Wragg (1992) that this remains a common approach today. It is still the case that many teachers base their teaching style on the model by which they were taught. In order to improve the skills of teachers of pupils with SEN, the recent emphasis on competence-based training courses and the increased use of action research techniques for the classroom teacher are positive developments.

COMPETENCE-BASED COURSES

Recently, attempts have been made by a variety of organisations involved in teacher training and professional development to analyse the key competences of effective classroom teachers in an attempt to identify and develop good practice. These competences are then set as tasks for trainee teachers to demonstrate their skills in these areas. This approach was given widespread approval by the Conservative Government at initial teaching level. Work on this approach has been done at both initial teacher training level, in-service training and Further Education (FE) (TDLB 1994).

In all these courses working with pupils with SEN has been incorporated into the competences to be achieved by students. Competences have also been specified for professional development courses for teachers who work with children with SEN. Such examples include competences specified by Hornby, Wickham and Zielinski (1990) and more recently by the Special Educational Needs Training Consortium (SENTC 1996).

The aim of SENTC (1996) is twofold. Firstly, they argue that a competences-based approach will aid the development of the professional skills of teachers of SEN. Secondly, they argue such an approach will provide a framework that will aid the measurement of quality assurance for SEN provision in schools. This has led to the development of lists of competences that identify the skills required by teachers as their involvement with those with SEN develops. SENTC (1996) have also taken into account the principles of competence-based training detailed by Hornby *et al* (1990) relating it to evidence that is authentic, current, sufficient and consistent across the detailed tasks.

The competences detailed by SENTC (1996) focus on the range of knowledge, skills, understanding and attitudes required by teachers to provide and manage effective education for pupils with SEN. These competences are set out in ten specific areas of disability. These include autism, emotional and behavioural difficulties, hearing impairment, language and communication difficulties, moderate learning difficulties, multi-sensory impairment, physical disabilities, severe learning difficulties, specific learning difficulties and visual impairment. Competences are also detailed for learning support teachers and SENCOs.

An analysis of these competences indicates that they can be identified with certain clearly identifiable roles. These can be divided into four categories: practical, organisational, liaison and personal. The practical roles include: demonstrating knowledge about the range of special needs and their educational implications, the use and evaluation of procedures for assessing pupils' needs, skills in creating, modifying or adapting teaching approaches and the skills of developing individual education plans for pupils.

Organisational roles deal with: work in carrying out responsibilities in relation to school and national policy requirements, advising other staff about prevention and intervention strategies for children experiencing a wide range of difficulties, the management of resources, equipment and materials, the management of both teaching and non-teaching staff working with children with SEN and co-ordinating and managing different levels of meetings to assess, evaluate and review pupils' needs.

The liaison role involves consulting with other staff in school in developing their knowledge, understanding and skills in this area of work, as well as sharing and exchanging knowledge and concerns with other professionals from outside the school. This role also takes into account the need to work in partnership with parents as well as developing sensitivity and empathy with pupils with SEN. All of these roles demand considerable interpersonal skills on behalf of the teacher, that will need to be developed as much as any of the other competencies detailed here.

The success of any competence-based scheme of personal development is in part related to the correct identification of those used in working situations, and the access of staff to situations where they can have the opportunity to demonstrate their skills and understanding. In many senses this is an approach that has been around as a basis for training through the national vocational qualification (NVQ) routes since 1986. However, in the more professional areas of work at levels 4 and 5 in the NVQ framework, its introduction has been fraught with difficulties.

For most teachers working in schools with pupils with SEN the NVQ approach is not too familiar. Its focus is on practical competences, the production of performance evidence to support claims for these and the portfolio approach to assessment. With respect to the first of these issues, SENTC (1996) clearly identified the range of competences needed in a wide range of circumstances by teachers working with pupils with SEN. In their entirety the competences listed, although useful as guidelines for teachers, are somewhat unwieldy and difficulties are likely to occur because of their repetitive nature across the specific areas listed.

It is debatable whether identifying and developing the full range of competences is a sound basis for all levels of professional development. There is a growing body of evidence that this approach has its own difficulties. Anecdotal evidence from the TDLB courses in initial teacher education in FE and from OFSTED (1996) with regard to GNVQ courses, which have a similar competence base, indicates some of these problems. These include: problems in relation to confusion over the interpretation of the requirements of the competences to be achieved. This relates particularly to the concept of 'minimum competence' and the training provided by the examination bodies to those developing such courses. Other difficulties include: linking the practical skills detailed to an understanding of the knowledge and awareness needed to successfully underpin them, wide variations in the quality and consistency of work produced to gain the award and difficulties in both the bureaucratic nature of the assessment process and the time needed to complete it. Further problems have been identified relating to the plagiarism and copying of work in portfolios of evidence presented by students on these courses.

Such difficulties have cast doubt on the integrity of competence-based training and has done little to inspire confidence in it. For it to be successful in the professional development of teachers, its execution and delivery must be of the highest quality and regular evaluations need to be made of both its effectiveness and emergent difficulties.

ACTION RESEARCH

The action research approach to professional development needs to be considered by teachers. This approach was initially developed in the UK by Stenhouse (1971) and others. It is set in a development cycle that has been detailed and discussed by Bell (1987), Bell *et al* (1984) and McNiff (1989). It is a research model which is suitable for individual use in classroom situations in promoting good practice. Its essentially flexible framework takes into account developments as the project is undertaken. Work documented by Bell *et al* (1994) demonstrates that this is particularly the case for teachers working with pupils with SEN. Beyond this, it is a suitable approach for collaborative activities by a group of teachers in one or more schools wishing to focus on a particular aspect of development.

The model can also serve as a useful practical introduction to classroom-based research activities. It allows for the planning and management of personal small-scale projects that are suited to individual needs. Further, it is being used extensively and with some success as part of the syllabus of award-bearing courses in post-qualification courses for teachers.

CONCLUSIONS

Throughout the last hundred years the role of the SEN specialist has grown and changed. The initial idea of such work being satisfactorily undertaken by the least qualified and most inexperienced teachers has been dispelled. Despite the low status often attached to the work it has encouraged the participation of many excellent teachers. Changes that have occurred in relation to the professional development of teachers in this field have moved from generally quite haphazard arrangements to a much more structured approach. Resources to further develop the skills and knowledge of teachers have throughout the century been a key issue, and continue to remain a problem.

However, despite these improvements, the most recent reports suggest that many teachers continue to feel a lack of confidence in working with pupils with SEN. Therefore the development of school based INSET courses organised by SEN co-ordinators and heads of department continue to be a necessity. The limited availability of appropriate award-bearing courses is a major concern at present. If this situation does not improve in the near future then the provision of effective teaching for pupils with SEN in mainstream schools will be threatened due to the lack of qualified SEN specialists. The introduction of competence-based approaches and the wider use of action research programmes by teachers are useful developments. At least these approaches, taken together, allow for the clearer identification of the various roles of specialist teachers and SENCOs as well as other staff working with pupils with SEN. Further, it will provide them with a suitable approach for developing their knowledge skills and understanding by putting them in a better position to analyse and reflect on their work.

Training opportunities have always lagged behind provision and have never been considered adequate to ensure enough qualified SEN specialists. Current gaps in the availability of training suggests that this situation is likely to continue, in the near future at least, and inadequate training opportunities have contributed towards inhibiting developments for pupils with SEN in mainstream schools.

Changing the management of SEN

(This chapter was written with the help of Christine Hogg)

INTRODUCTION

A key factor in the process of change in the organisation of educational provision, for all children in mainstream schools and not only those with SEN, is its management. This is a key factor in the development of provision throughout the whole school. The management of change entails the change of behaviour, as Mintzberg and Quinn indicate:

> whether we realise it or not, our behaviour is guided by the systems of ideas that we have internalised over the years. Much can be learned by bringing these out into the open, examining them more carefully and comparing them with alternative ways to view the world – including ones based on a systematic study (that is research).
>
> Mintzberg and Quinn (1991, p. xii)

The teaching profession, at home with learning theories, is perhaps better equipped than most for change. Given the relevant information, professional commitment, appropriate organisation and resource allocation it is possible that a great deal could be achieved in this area.

The guidelines available regarding the management of SEN provision in mainstream schools has focused on particular issues. Historically, the more important of these have been concerned with curriculum selection, classroom management and the development of the role of teachers responsible for pupils with SEN.

As far as the management of SEN provision is concerned there are other critical issues which need to be addressed. These include financial and human resource management. The purpose of this chapter is to analyse implications for the management of provision for SEN in mainstream schools with these two features in mind. This will be done taking account of an historical perspective in order to identify some of the changes which can be identified in the management of pupils with SEN provision in mainstream schools.

FINANCIAL MANAGEMENT

One of the key factors in determining the financing of SEN in mainstream schools has been the tension between central government funding and local demands. As detailed in Chapter Two, major difficulties have arisen over the years in the provision of sufficient finance to meet the recommendations of the various committees and commissions that have reported and made recommendations to Parliament. It has been suggested that lack of financial commitment regarding SEN provision has been related to a distinct lack of the political will necessary to bring about the desired changes.

Further, when changes that have needed a financial input have been proposed by official reports and committees these seem to have coincided with downturns in the overall economic climate. This was particularly the case with the Wood Report (1929), to some extent after the 1944 Act and also during the period after the 1981 Education Act.

These financial problems have, in their turn, led to difficulties with staffing policy for pupils with SEN. It has generally been the case at times of economic stringency that staffing for pupils with SEN, particularly those in the mainstream school, has been cut first. At times of more favourable economic circumstances they have not always been the first to be restored. Comparisons can be made with the resourcing models in some other European countries and the USA described by Booth (1982) and O'Hanlon (1993), where the amount of money invested and the overall arrangements made for similar children appear much more favourable than in England and Wales.

The overall situation with regard to the resourcing of SEN provision has led to a vicious circle of events in which lack of resources has led to a lack of planning which, in turn, has led to a lack of overall strategy for provision. As a consequence, this has led to wide national variations in the provision that has been made.

Problems with adequate resourcing for pupils with SEN have existed since the introduction of compulsory education. Initially, this can be related to a number of key points. These include: a lack of the basic knowledge of individual children's SEN and effective intervention strategies to make the necessary provision, the lack of political will to bring about effective provision, which has been discussed earlier in this book and an overall lack of planning and co-ordination of appropriate arrangements for pupils with SEN at the national level.

Despite the committees initiated by governments in the early part of the century, no overall resourcing strategy was in place, and provision was largely based on local conditions and circumstances. The Wood Report (1929) was the first to have a remit to investigate the prevalence of children with SEN and provision and resources for them. Unfortunately, as mentioned earlier, the publication of the Wood Report in 1929 identified ambitious plans that would need a considerable increase in financial outlay, and also coincided with the worldwide economic depression and domestic economic slump. This produced not only considerable financial hardship for individual families, but also for governments of the period.

Because of the overall national economic position, the 1920s and 1930s were decades of severe financial restriction throughout the whole of the education service. Provision for pupils with SEN, which was not regarded as a national economic priority, suffered in the same way as the rest of the service. As such there was no budget allocated to finance any of the recommendations of the Wood Report (1929). Its influence was rather as a marker for future policy developments. This can be seen in particular in the recommendations of the Hadow Report (1936) and the Spens Report (1938), which implicitly acknowledged some of the points raised by the Wood Committee.

THE POST-WAR PERIOD

In the period after the 1944 Education Act more money was made available for the education programme and a larger percentage of the Gross National Product (GNP) was set aside for this purpose. Some of this money was directed specifically towards children with SEN in the categories detailed in the 1994 Act. This was particularly the case for children in special schools. However, for pupils with SEN in mainstream schools, the destination of the money was not clearly defined, nor was any real check kept on how it was being used. The money was distributed as part of schools' overall annual capitation. As Sayer (1989) indicated, the distribution of the annual capitation was left largely to the head teacher. From this point of view SEN provision was largely reliant on the patronage of head teachers, the influence which could be brought to bear on them and their perceptions of the need for SEN provision.

FINANCING CHANGE

Financing the required changes was a major issue in the post-Warnock era. This was particularly the case during the period between the passing of the Education Act in 1981 and its implementation on 1 April 1983. Initially, pressure was put on the government to finance those parts of the Act which fell outside the normal education budget. This was accompanied by considerable government reluctance. Baroness Young (1980), while acknowledging the argument for extra resources, expressed considerable doubt about the view that nothing could be changed without increased funding. In denying this she indicated that some of the money needed during the next five-year period would be made available through the overall drop in the national birth-rate. A consequence of this, she argued, would be a drop in the number of pupils needing special help!

Lukes (1981) claimed that the 1981 Act provided more scope for spending cuts in special educational provision, particularly through the focus on integration. In her view this has been a deliberate policy initiated by governments. She argued that reductions in the Rate Support Grant (RSG) from 1976 made this inevitable. Further, she indicated that as the integration of pupils with SEN into mainstream schools was a cheaper option than provision in separate special schools, LEAs would increasingly be forced to look at this as a realistic option. Such an approach Lukes (1981) indicated would lead to an unevenness in the cuts which were made in different LEAs. The LEAs which would be hardest hit would be those in urban areas in which there was often the greatest need for SEN provision.

It is the case that SEN provision is more expensive than that for the rest of the pupils in mainstream schools. Lukes (1981) identified a number of reasons for this. These included the smaller pupil–teacher ratio and the cost of teacher-aides and transport costs as well as the cost of teachers' salaries. At a time of increasing financial stringency and cost cutting these are important factors which need to be taken into account when looking at the overall costs involved.

Given the demand-led model of provision of the time, the Warnock Report (1978) made it clear that their recommendations could not be implemented without some financial input from both national and local government sources. The areas where they indicated this was most needed were in curriculum innovation, in-service education for staff development and in changes to premises to allow better access and accommodation, thereby increasing the integration of pupils with SEN into mainstream schools. The report, taking into account the widespread changes which would be needed, acknowledged that these recommendations would have to bear in mind the need for qualifying conditions. These were set in terms of practicability, efficiency and cost.

Practicability was seen in terms of the quality of provision, the availability and adaptation that could be made to existing buildings and the travelling costs of the pupils to attend the schools which had modifications made to them. The definition of efficiency reflected the contemporary educational thinking of the period. The Report saw this in terms of the efficiency of instruction and teaching which could be provided in the school through the development of good practice. The Report indicated that efficiency could be dealt with from four different viewpoints: the physical organisation of the school, curriculum planning, the emotional needs of pupils and the knowledge and ability of the teaching staff.

The question of financing the recommendations was particularly vague in the Report. No attempt was made by the Warnock Committee to price the different recommendations they had made. It was considered by the Committee that finances would be made available by Parliament. This, perhaps somewhat naively, was based on the view that as it was Parliament which had initiated the work of the Committee in the first place, they would also be prepared to resource its recommendations. What the report did make clear was that any costs must be part of an overall plan by LEAs, based on the national education budget. Integration, it was argued, must not be seen as a cheap alternative to placement in special schools.

While the accusation of financial naiveté might be raised against the Warnock Report, it did express views regarding how and where funding should come from. It also indicated that a financial realignment would be a necessary part of the re-structuring process. This was a point supported by Burnham (1982) and Booth (1982) who argued that LEAs must prioritise their decisions and deploy what money was available accordingly.

Even with the financial redistribution detailed above the Warnock Committee, taking into account the widespread changes which they had called for, argued that there could be no meaningful implementation of its recommendations without some extra financial input. The Warnock Committee expected more resources to be put at the disposal of LEAs and individual schools than was in fact forthcoming. The Report recognised that certain of its key proposals would need substantial additional expenditure in the long term. Jones (1983), Potts (1982a) and Burden (1985) all argued that the restriction on resources imposed severe difficulties on schools attempting to implement the required changes. Bookbinder (1981) concurred, arguing that schools were failing to provide adequately for the majority of pupils, let alone those with special needs. Further, he suggested, they could not be expected to meet the needs of the least able and those with disabilities, who required additional staffing resources, for which extra finance was unavailable.

Particular criticisms were raised of the overall direction of the financing of the 1981 Act from the various teacher unions. The NUT (1980), while implicitly supporting the Warnock philosophy, demanded more resources to implement it. A similar position was taken by the NAS/UWT (1983). Further documentation from the NAS/UWT (1986) indicated that, in the period after 1983, few extra resources had in fact been committed to this area. The HMI/Audit Commission Report (DES 1992) however indicated that some of these resources were not being used efficiently, and that there was a considerable disparity between the spending of LEAs on SEN provision.

In the decade after the implementation of the 1981 Act there was growing evidence that the increasing financial restraints imposed by central government in an effort to cut back on its public borrowing were having a negative effect on provision at local level. In the same period the number of pupils regarded as having SEN as well as those with statements increased. Figures from Evans and Lunt (1993) showed that there had been an increase in the same period of the overall school population who had received statements. The returns indicated that from 2 per cent of the population in this category in 1990, the figures rose to 2.2 per cent in 1991 and 2.4 per cent in 1992. Davie (1996) indicated this had recently risen to 3 per cent on the school population. Berliner (1993) indicated that there had been a large increase in the number of pupils statemented in the period between 1983 and 1991. This was supported by figures produced by Evans and Lunt (1993) which indicated that LEA returns in the period since the publication of the Warnock Report had produced an 84 per cent increase in the number of pupils statemented.

Evidence collected by The Spastics Society (1992) indicated that, as far as pupils with SEN were concerned, the greatest problem facing LEAs was a lack of funding to make the necessary provision. Warnock (1993) indicated similarly, commenting that despite the changes which had occurred local authorities continued to make decisions about pupils with SEN based on the resources at their disposal rather than on the needs of individual pupils. High quality SEN provision was still relatively low priority in LEA spending as central government continued to increase control using fiscal means.

The Audit Commission/HMI Report (1992) supported the view that the finance and the provision available varied in different LEAs.

They indicated that there were two areas where widespread discrepancies could be found. The first was between the number of statements of SEN which had been made in different LEAs where their research had been conducted. The second was the varying lengths of time it took different LEAs to prepare statements. It was this latter feature which led to a considerable number of complaints from both parents and teachers over this issue.

Warnock (1993) saw the statementing procedure and its increasingly important links to extra finance for pupils as an area of developing tensions. She argued that the sheer volume of pupils to be statemented and the financial pressures which this had created were important contributory factors to this. A recent report (Coopers and Lybrand, 1997) indicates that spending on SEN provision has emerged as a key issue for LEAs, with costs rising to 12.5 per cent of their school budget. Financing SEN provision has risen in line with the number of statements prepared for children with SEN. The report also suggests that by the turn of the century some 5 per cent of children be in receipt of an SEN statement. This, it argues, will create a serious funding crisis, where the needs of the majority of children may be penalised. Pyke (1996) reported that the situation is reaching breaking point and that the country is faced with a moral dilemma which is in urgent need of a political solution.

HUMAN RESOURCE MANAGEMENT

Torrington and Weightman (1988) argued that traditionally the core professional task of teachers had been to manage their relationship with children. Special educational provision has largely concentrated on this aspect of management. However, in recent years the focus of management in schools for those working with children with SEN has expanded to a much wider constituency of children, parents, advisers and teachers. Everard (1984) set effective school management in relation to three key factors. These were the management of all those who worked there, the management of the organisation of which they formed a part and the successful management of change within it. These factors, he argued, must be taken into account in any strategies which are adopted to improve the standards of teaching and learning for all pupils.

Models for the management of education are largely derived from industrial experience. Cubberly (1916) indicated that school management was crude and simplistic, concentrating extensively on industrial needs and social control. He portrayed education as having its own 'efficiency experts' and schools 'as building a product according to specifications which have already been laid down' (p. 388).

In the UK the management of the mainstream school is complex. Approaches to this have been greatly influenced by classical management theories with the emphasis on the control function of management. This approach has led to the common use of the bureaucratic principles described by Weber (1947). Weber's principles stress the role of 'office', procedures, the division of labour and the need for hierarchy. These can be identified in the traditional approach to management espoused by many schools. The human relationship approach associated with Mayo (1933) and highly relevant to a professional organisation, does not appear to have had a major impact on the operation of organisational structures within schools. Furthermore, the concept and power of strategic management (Mintzberg 1973) has sadly been unappreciated. Essentially schools have had difficulties in grasping the basic requirements of their organisational model, being neither truly bureaucratic on the one hand nor able to effectively use the strategic planning model described by Mintzberg (1973).

The management of provision for pupils with SEN has not been a major priority in the mainstream school. Sayer (1987) and Salmon and Poster (1988) pointed out that until comparatively recently it had received little attention. Jones and Southgate (1989) claimed that until recently head teachers have had few guidelines to help them tackle the issues involved. Sayer (1987) and Salmon and Poster (1988) also indicated that it was only in recent years that management courses for head teachers had attempted to address the management of SEN.

Jones and Southgate (1989) argued that there are two structures of management within the school system: one related to the promotion of academic achievement and the other concerned with personal and social development. For pupils within mainstream schools the main focus is on academic achievement, while special schools are more concerned with personal and social education with a strong emphasis on pastoral care. In their view, the management of SEN within the mainstream school is often seen as a separate and distinct activity from that of other pupils.

Historically, the separation of the management of SEN provision from that of the rest of the school can be most easily identified in the secondary school. This is particularly the case where the school has employed streaming or banding as a mechanism for the organisation of pupils by ability. In such circumstances the bottom stream, or in larger schools, the bottom two or three streams are identified in this way. This has led to the pupils in these streams, through their identification as having different needs encompassing both academic and pastoral features, requiring a different management style. Further, it is the case that in schools which have adopted streaming or banding, the decision to place pupils in SEN departments is determined more by logistical factors surrounding the number of children which must be placed in a class with a teacher than addressing their individual needs.

Jones and Southgate (1989) argued that the twin structure of management within the mainstream school has led to the development of dual standards for pupils. In their view pupils with SEN have had to meet different, generally less exacting, standards from the rest of their peer group. Further, Jones and Southgate (1989) identified a number of areas where they asserted this was the case. These related particularly to standards of teaching for pupils with SEN, the expectation of such pupils by their teachers and to levels of professionalism between those staff working with these children and the rest of the staff in the school.

It is generally agreed that the moves towards the greater integration of pupils with more complex special needs into mainstream schools has increased management difficulties. Jones and Southgate (1989), Sayer (1989), Walters (1994) and Fish and Evans (1995) all argued that the management of integration was being undertaken through inappropriate strategies. Each of these writers has indicated that the management of SEN in mainstream schools must be an integral part of overall school management.

The use of the concept of good practice is widely used and it is commonly associated with a number of professional development issues on both an individual and school-wide basis. However, much of its true meaning remains implicit to the individual or is taken for granted. Essentially, it can be argued, the phrase 'good practice' is concerned with good management and it is from this perspective that changes and developments occur.

Walters (1994) asserted that the management of SEN includes the relationship between three factors. These are: the concepts of beliefs and values held by society regarding the needs of children with SEN, ideas relating to the quality of the provision which is made for them, and the planning of policies which occur as a consequence of these. He has argued that good management is largely dependent on the development of sound policies. This has to be undertaken at all levels of administration. For the management of SEN in mainstream schools this must occur three levels: at DfEE, LEA and individual school levels. Further, Walters (1994) asserted that to be successful, not only is it necessary to produce coherent policies at all administrative levels but also there needs to be a common consensus on them at each of these stages.

Policy and planning which is undertaken must take into account the three stages described by Walters (1994) and view the provision of SEN as a sub-system contained within the open system of education, influenced by and contributing to, the external and internal environment of economy, work and society. This entails the development of objectives encapsulated in a vision, underpinned by a mission statement and a strategic plan.

THE CURRENT POSITION

Throughout the century, the pace of the management of change of SEN provision has been frustratingly slow. Some might consider that given the four dominant themes of political will, societal influence, financial provision and resource management, the nature of change is going to be incremental rather than radical, evolutionary rather than revolutionary (Mintzberg and Quinn 1991). The evidence detailed earlier in the book indicates that conflicts between these themes have led to an overall lack of direction and frustration on the part of teachers and parents of children with SEN.

A recent example of these difficulties can be seen in the OFSTED Report (1996). The survey reported positively that some headway has been made since the introduction of the Code of Practice (1994) in both special and mainstream schools. The developments noted included: better staff awareness of the issues relating to SEN, significant improvements in planning and provision, more effective strategies for the identification and assessment of pupils, developments in the use of IEPs and target-setting relating to each school-based stage of the Code, better documentation at the point of requesting external support at Stage 3 and at the time of statutory assessment at Stage 4. The Report further indicated increased attention being paid in the School Development Plan to SEN. Nevertheless, despite these positive factors, the Report also identified twelve key improvements which schools needed to consider, including both strategic and operational issues.

Developments have also occurred in societal attitudes to children with SEN in recent years. These are best exemplified in the increasing emphasis on the overall rights of mankind and awareness of equal opportunities issues. Equality of opportunity is now seen as a fundamental part of a democratic society. Organisations are required by law to demonstrate their commitment to both the principle and the practice of equality of opportunity. Equal opportunities and the value of the individual is a theme in all teacher training programmes and teachers in mainstream schools have become increasingly knowledgeable in how to work positively with the growing number of pupils with complex and sometimes multiple difficulties. Nevertheless, there is still a long way to go before those with SEN can be considered to be fully participative in a society which values them as equals.

The values attached to the education of and participation within schools by children with SEN has been an area of considerable debate. Despite recent developments, changes in societal values have evolved slowly throughout the century. Such changes have been mirrored by changes in the management of provision. An example of this was provided by Stewart and Ranson (1988) who pointed out that moves within society towards a greater equality of opportunity for pupils with SEN and their placement in mainstream schools has influenced the management of provision made for them.

Current developments within wider society indicates that the movement continues to be towards their greater social acceptability of children with SEN. From this point of view mainstream schools will have to take this into account in organising the provision which is to be made. It is now much more likely than at any time in the history of mainstream schools children with complex special educational needs will be admitted to mainstream schools.

Walters (1994) argued that the values held by society must be seen not only in terms of beliefs and ideals which are held but also in terms of actions which can be taken to aid good management. It is essential that the philosophical, moral and ethical values held by a society towards children with SEN are translated into practical management strategies which can be put in place and evaluated. Questions focusing on such practical issues relating to SEN have been raised recently by Walters (1994), Evans and Lunt (1994) and Fish and Evans (1995).

Fish and Evans (1995) questioned the development of policy at all levels in the administration. Their concerns included: the decentralisation of educational provision to local management, the influence of the concept of value for money in education, the greater influence of customer-led activities and the imposition of increasing financial restraints on available resources.

As detailed in Chapter Two, increasingly the articulate voices of powerful lobby groups, while promoting equality of opportunity on a broad political front, have failed to take into account the overall resource implications. Political commitment is ineffective without careful consideration of these implications. Inadequate attention to these vital aspects inevitably leads to weak and inconsistent policy implementation. Successful implementation relies upon developing expertise at all levels. Some initiatives are currently in place but will take time to have an impact upon SEN provision. For example, the Headlamp Programme and the National Professional Qualification for Headship (NPQH 1996).

Despite the influence of the 1981 and 1993 Education Acts on equal opportunities legislation, the evidence indicates that although the integrationist lobby has strengthened its position in recent years and developments have occurred through equal rights legislation, the operational management of these policies within schools for pupils with SEN remains less than satisfactory. Overall, national provision for pupils with SEN continues to be patchy and is strongly influenced by individual values and beliefs at the organisational level. The evidence indicates that any policy is only as successful as its implementation and successful policy implementation requires the formulation of clearly thought out strategies.

Increasingly, finances are seen as finite and the demand led model of provision for SEN is regarded as inappropriate, even burdensome. Strategies within the educational service have increasingly had to operate within tight financial constraints both in the present and for the foreseeable future. Therefore, financial considerations have had an impact upon strategic implementation. Fish and Evans (1995) have argued that SEN provision is no different since it must operate within the same financial constraints. This impacts upon the pace of strategic implementation but not upon strategic direction. In terms of working towards a comprehensive educational provision for those with special needs, it is strategic direction which is of major importance. It is a perceived lack of progress in a specific direction which is demotivating.

Opportunities for progress have been provided by the Warnock Report, the Code of Practice and the recent Professional Development Initiatives. But it appears that at the operational level there is as yet no clear vision to work towards.

Resource management is yet another factor affecting the operationalisation of policy. Ensuring maximum utilisation of current resources and planning for further development and sustainability of resources is an integral part of policy implementation. The efficient use of current resources and the development of future resources gives credibility to any strategy. It leads to acceptance, relevance and ownership of the strategy. A strategy cannot work in a vacuum. In SEN provision, this includes both tangible and intangible resources. It is important that these are utilised as effectively as possible.

Tangible resources include teaching materials and research, both quantitative and qualitative, on the teaching and learning strategies of pupils with SEN. There is a growing body of knowledge, through the work of Bowers (1985), Walters (1994) and Jones and Southgate (1989), on the organisational aspects of special needs provision which also needs to facilitate and inform strategy implementation.

Intangible resources include the goodwill and personal commitment of many, both inside and outside the teaching profession, to improve the current provision. Inside the profession, teachers develop specific skills which frequently are lost to others following them on their departure from their teaching and supporting position. This leakage represents an enormous loss of resources which must be addressed in a systematic and planned way. Professional associations have been working on this for many years. The systems for sharing this knowledge base may be increasingly enhanced by the use of the Internet and telecommunications.

THE FUTURE

National strategies for SEN provision need to be guided by a shared vision incorporating overriding objectives for LEAs and individual schools to work towards, thus facilitating further developments for high-quality provision by experienced practitioners.

Within schools management systems, and therefore strategies, need to take into account two key groups: pupils with SEN and the staff who work with them. The last few years have indeed seen the development of relevant strategies. The definition of the role of the SEN department by NARE (1979) and SENTC (1996) are examples of this, as was the introduction of the Code of Practice (1994).

The educational programme, for up to one in five of the school population, must be more appropriate than that currently provided by the academically orientated content of the National Curriculum or a programme of teaching basic skills to allow children merely to cope. The aim must be for quality of experience and quality of life. Pupils with SEN need to be encouraged to think they can achieve more than they first thought, take a pride in and enjoy coming to school and have commitment to their personal development. Planning must therefore ensure that the situation is seen in terms of the need to modify teaching strategies in a non-threatening way, rather than as an indication of the innate disability of the child. This will involve the development of counselling skills so that pupils may better realise their potential and be enabled to play a greater role in the decisions which are made about their education.

The skill base would be enhanced by the development of a learning skills centre which would create a databank of appropriate learning materials made accessible by a network of information systems. This would represent a core of professional expertise essential for high quality INSET provision. Networking would also encourage and facilitate co-operative learning, thus continuing the development of professional expertise and knowledge. Much work is still needed on SEN in a particular curriculum context, and the dissemination of such knowledge would be a vital role for SEN staff and the learning skills centre.

The future for SEN must involve the definition of quality provision in an organisation, the development of procedures and realistic performance indicators to be implemented in a non-punitive manner. The teaching profession prides itself on critical reflection as an essential component of the achievement of high-quality provision. However, the quality of reflection depends upon a base knowledge for comparison and values. Increased awareness of SEN teaching and learning strategies and support mechanisms is therefore essential to improve the quality of special needs provision.

Providers are constantly revisiting teaching/learning strategies and learning materials. Embedding SEN as priority in the learning provision requires the participation of those involved in the learning process. This could be done through professional development associations networked through professional associations. Drucker (1973) argued that if objectives are only good intentions, they are worthless. He pointed out that work always has or should have unambiguous, measurable results, a deadline and a specific assignment of responsibility.

Current planning and policy-making has to take these factors, as well as those relating to a greater equality of opportunity and the greater integration of pupils with SEN into mainstream schools, into account when planning and drawing up policies for children with SEN. Currently, educational planning often involves the production of mission statements to incorporate overall values and aims. Mission statements for SEN have been developed at all levels of its administration. Examples of these at the national level include statutory instruments; at LEA level, LEA guidelines and at individual school level, work undertaken by Gordon (1992) and the Audit Commission (1992b). Further examples can be identified at a political level through the production of pamphlets and policy statements on SEN policy by the major political parties.

An analysis of mission statements for SEN provision and development at all management levels indicates that these are largely composed of four elements. These are concerned with: educational entitlement, the integration of pupils with SEN, the quality of provision which is made for them and performance-related outcomes which are both achievable and measurable.

It is through the setting and measurement of the achievement of these targets that progress is ascertained and further developments are decided. There continues to be a wide variation in the instruments which are used to measure progress throughout the system. One increasingly common instrument to assist with this has been developed by the British Standards Institution (BS 5750). This approach incorporates a number of useful evaluative tools. These include a review of the policy under scrutiny, a measurement of the development of a corporate attitude to gauge the active participation of all staff and a focus on the particular needs of an institution.

STRATEGIC ASPECTS

The key to the future appears to be in the development of a comprehensive strategy for SEN in schools. Without a strategy little of major significance is likely to be achieved. Strategy, inevitably, is a reflection of the attitudes, beliefs, values and expectations of those with influence. Consequently changes are slow in coming. Mintzberg and Quinn (1991) indicated the need for critical reflection. There must be a clear rationale for change, evidenced by research, for great conviction is needed for a strategy leading to major change. Johnson and Scholes (1984) explored the tripartite relationship between strategic analysis, strategic choice and strategic implementation. All three elements are essential to the development of provision for children with SEN in mainstream schools.

Strategic analysis involves a close investigation of the past, current and future trends of the environmental factors affecting the policy and its implementation. Careful consideration and estimation of variables such as economic, political, technological, ethical and social factors are essential to assessing the potential pace and direction of change. From time to time there may be windows of opportunity which will facilitate incremental change. Accurate information as to the resources available and those required for implementation of the strategy need to be researched at length. Skills audits and up-dating training give a snapshot of the current situation. However, skilled personnel leave, frequently taking their expertise with them. In addition, training for the unmotivated results in zero increase of skill base. The situation is complex: people are complex and managing change is about changing the behaviour of people.

APPROACHES TO CHANGE MANAGEMENT

Over the years various conflicting theories and approaches to managing change have emerged, many of which were devised to meet the needs of a particular organisation. It has been argued earlier in this chapter that the effective management of SEN provision must be seen as an integral part of that of the whole school. In this respect it is appropriate to discuss some of the possible approaches which may help such developments.

The theory and practice of change management draws on a number of social science disciplines. The interdisciplinary nature of change management is one of its strengths, but it does complicate discussion. There are three major schools of thought which inform the debate on change management theory. The *individual perspective* school, as its name suggests, focuses on the individual. Within this school there two approaches: the Behaviourists and the Gestalt-Field Psychologists. Both approaches are influential in the management of change where strong individual incentives (external stimuli) and genuine participation (internal reflection) may be used to bring about organisational change. (Peters and Waterman 1982).

The *Human Relations* school (Maslow 1943, Hertzberg and Mayo 1931) emphasised the need for both external and internal stimuli to influence behaviour, but it also concentrates on the behaviour of individuals in groups. The Group Dynamics school (Schein 1969, Bernstein 1968, Lewin 1958) analyses the effect of group practices and norms on individual behaviour. Kurt Lewin (1958) argued that individual behaviour is affected by the group environment producing tensions in each of the group members. Thus, to bring about change, the groups norms, roles and values must be influenced as any single group member is constrained by group pressures to conform (French and Bell 1984, Cummings and Huse 1989, Smith 1985). This school of thought has influenced the practice of change management, indeed the Investors In People Quality Award (IIP) depends upon viewing organisations being comprised of a number of small interweaving (overlapping) teams (Mullins 1989). French and Bell (1984) also emphasised the role of teams in developing strategies to increase efficiency and effectiveness in the organisation.

The *Open Systems* school (Tavistock Institute 1970) views the organisation holistically, interacting with the external environment and with interdependent subsystems operating in a network. Butler (1985) argues that one of the difficulties of this approach is that systems involving people are extremely complex and dynamic, which makes analysis difficult. Cause-and-effect relationships are problematic to sort out. Several key theorists support the Systems school of thought (e.g. Burnes and Stalker 1961, Woodward 1965, Lawrence and Lorsch 1967).

These three schools of thought together inform the management of the change process. As detailed earlier in discussions on curricular change in Chapter Five, to change anything requires both the co-operation and consent of the groups and individuals in an organisation. It is only through their behaviour that abstract organisational concepts are realised in terms of structures, systems, procedures and technologies.

MODELS OF ORGANISATIONAL CHANGE

Despite the number of different approaches there are three basic models of the change process which emerged from the work of Kurt Lewin (1958) which may be appropriate for developing provision for pupils with SEN in mainstream schools. These three models of the change process are: The Action Research model, the 3-Step model and the Phases of Planned Change model. There are similarities to these models of change, but the main difference between the approaches is that of the involvement of the people who are required to change. The Action Research model requires the involvement of the individuals (teams, teachers) who are expected to change, with the assistance of a change agent (SEN co-ordinator). The 3-Step and Planned models require less involvement of the people who are expected to change, placing more responsibility on the external or internal change agent to provide solutions for them to accept.

Whichever model of change is used, there is a need to change the way in which individuals or groups behave in order to provided good-quality SEN experience in schools. Many difficulties are experienced if the full participation of practitioners is not a key part of the change process.

MANAGING CHANGE

Management in the 1990s is about managing change. Successful strategic management, considers the qualitative rather than the quantitative aspects of change since change involves people and therefore social processes. People need to be convinced of the need for change. They need a long term goal, a vision encapsulated in a mission, or strategic purpose, valued outcomes, preferred conditions to achieve change, and phased targets to meet along the path to the vision (Cummings and Huse 1989). Is there yet a vision for SEN provision in mainstream schools? Are there interim objectives for staff to work towards?

Strategic planning for change means phases, deadlines and evaluation against performance indicators. What indicators should be used, and who should select appropriate indicators? Successful change inevitably means the full participation of the teachers affected by the planning and implementation of change. Only the process of genuine consultation and participation will ensure the necessary change of behaviour required for successful change at all levels: individual, group, school, LEA and DfEE. Cultural change is an essential element of the management of change

Burnes (1992) identified nine elements constituting a new approach to the change process. Four elements create the conditions which allow successful change to take place: a vision, strategies, creating a readiness for change, and the right culture. Successful change requires cultures which encourage flexibility, autonomy and teamwork, not qualities frequently found in the traditional mainstream school. Handy (1986) indicates that change is less likely to be successful if the culture and the organisation structure are inflexible.

The other five elements are the phases needed for successful change: assessing the need for change, planning and implementing, involvement, sustaining the momentum and continuous improvement. Considerable managerial skill is thus required for management today, skills which need developing, skills which may not be present in some schools.

CONCLUSIONS

The management of pupils with SEN in mainstream schools has historically been seen as separate to that of the rest of the pupils in the school. Such an approach has created difficulties which have increased considerably in recent years with the integration of pupils with a wider range of disabilities into the schools.

The financial management of SEN provision has changed from a largely demand-led model to one which is resource-based. This change has increased frustrations in the same way that there has been constant frustration with provision being regarded as a prime target for cuts at times of economic difficulties.

The situation in the UK with respect to the management of SEN provision is no different from that in other countries. Booth (1982c) pointed out that provision in the USA was dependent on state, rather than federal decisions. He described a familiar pattern, of decisions relating to local interpretations of the law and a willingness to make provision. Similar comments have been identified about provision in

Italy, by O'Hanlon (1993) and in Greece (Bardis 1993) where the level and type of provision for those with SEN is largely dependent on where one lives.

For real changes to be made these need to be set in a vision for SEN provision. This must include overall policy in this area, its provision and practice. For change to be sustained the development of appropriate management strategies is critical. The lack of such strategies over the past hundred years has been a major factor in retarding progress in the development of effective and appropriate climate for SEN provision in mainstream schools.

Conclusions

INTRODUCTION

The evidence presented throughout this book shows that progress regarding provision for pupils with SEN in mainstream schools throughout the period of compulsory education has been dependent on the seven factors which have been identified as making up the cartwheel model. These factors have acted as controlling mechanisms, with varying degrees of influence, on the nature and direction of provision for pupils with SEN in mainstream schools.

Some of these factors are directly related to provision made for pupils with SEN, while others are concerned with aspects of the education service as a whole or to attitudes and values in the wider society. It is the attitudes of the wider society with regard to such things as the social and economic value of people with SEN which most strongly influence decisions which are made about provisions for SEN pupils. These values impinge on subsequent political decisions which are taken and the level of resourcing which is made available to maintain and develop provision.

This is a complex situation. Each of the seven factors which have been identified operates in two dimensions. Individually they can be seen to have their own dynamics and their discrete conflicts and tensions. However, each of these areas cannot be taken as individual, discrete and in isolation from each other Change in the development of SEN provision in mainstream schools is also dependent on the association between each of these factors and the tensions which can be identified between them. This relationship creates collective tensions which have to be addressed by policy-makers and planners at all levels in the administration of SEN. The relationship between each of the seven factors also act as a framework in which the compromises which influence the overall direction and pace of policy for pupils with SEN in mainstream schools is determined.

Bearing these points in mind, this concluding chapter will focus firstly on analysing some of the debates on the individual factors, secondly it will focus on discussing the effects of these collectively on the overall development which has taken place in provision for pupils with SEN in mainstream schools.

THE FIRST DIMENSION

Integration

The question of the integration of pupils with SEN into mainstream schools has been a major feature of the debates on SEN provision throughout the whole period of compulsory education. For much of the period these debates have led to indecision over the best direction of policy. As a consequence, provision within mainstream schools has been left in a state of disarray, with different points of view influencing policy in different parts of the country, and consequent variations in the development of provision. Since the 1981 Education Act the inclusive lobby has been increasingly dominant in developments which have occurred and the integration of pupils with SEN into mainstream schools has been accepted much more widely in society.

This changing attitude to integration has been brought about through a variety of different influences beyond those directly concerned with the education service. These can be related particularly to the changes in social and political thinking in our society. Those factors which have most clearly influenced thinking on integration include: changes in the moral and ethical position regarding disability in society, wider awareness of human rights and a greater acknowledgement of equal opportunities. Each of these factors has influenced changes in provision. This has been the case particularly in relation to the views of parents of children with SEN who have campaigned for changes which have led to a wider acceptance of both the educational and social value of placing children with SEN in mainstream schools. Increasingly throughout the century, this pressure has influenced the policy regarding pupils with SEN and has led to changes in both provision and practice.

Provision of resources

The provision of resources for pupils with SEN is dependent on both social and political factors. This has been an area of considerable difficulty throughout the whole period of compulsory schooling. These difficulties have come as a result of tensions between the expectations of parents and teachers on the one hand, and politicians and administrators on the other. A number of influences have been identified as important in this respect. Most important among these has been tension between the resource-based and the demand-led models of funding and the increasing demands on available resources.

For much of the period the demand-led model of funding has been dominant in the thinking and expectations of both teachers and parents of children with SEN. Both of these groups have had high expectations of resources being made available to meet the needs of these pupils.

Increasingly, medical knowledge about children with SEN has ensured that a larger number have a longer life expectancy than was previously the case. Further, an increasing number of children with SEN are being placed in mainstream schools. As a consequence, more resources have been needed to accommodate them and successfully meet their needs. An increase in resources to meet these changes has not been forthcoming. This has led to the increasing frustration of both parents and teachers.

This increased need for resources has been compounded by developments in the techniques used to identify pupils with difficulties both before they arrive at school as well as through the use of more sophisticated assessment techniques in schools. Implementation of the Code of Practice has led to a greater proportion of pupils being identified by schools as having SEN. This has led to increasing pressure on the availability of resources. These factors have put greater pressures on the demand led model of provision. This has produced two areas of difficulty. Firstly, an increased expectation by parents and teachers in recent years which has resulted in increasing reliance on legal intervention. Secondly, more recent difficulties have led to demands from certain quarters for greater reliance on a resource-based model of funding provision for children with SEN in mainstream schools. It is considered that these developments will lead to further conflict between the providers and users.

Political will
The tensions outlined above relating to the resourcing of SEN are, in part, a result of political activity. Political decisions have had, and continue to have, a considerable influence on the pace and direction of SEN provision and policy. Through much of the period of compulsory education there has consistently been a lack of political commitment to meeting the educational needs of pupils with SEN. As a result there has been a lack of overall vision in this area and the necessary planning to bring about meaningful change has stuttered through a lack of clear overall direction and drive from politicians. Until relatively recently this situation has pertained not only at national level but also through

the relationship which exists between central and local government. On occasions this has led to inaction rather than development and reflected an overall lack of political will towards improving provision for children with SEN in the mainstream school.

The status of children with SEN has remained discouragingly low in mainstream schools for much of the period since the introduction of compulsory education. Until the time of the 1981 Education Act there were few attempts towards a national policy which would initiate appropriate educational development. Throughout the century many of the changes in SEN provision have been made as a result of the enactment of wider legislation for all pupils in mainstream schools. However, with the 1993 Act and the Code of Practice, there is at last comprehensive guidance on the components of effective provision for pupils with SEN in mainstream schools.

Social influences
Changes within wider society have created their own tensions in relation to provision for pupils with SEN. Some of the more important issues have already been discussed in relation to acceptance of the need for increased integration of children with SEN in mainstream schools. Throughout the period of compulsory schooling there has been an increasingly more positive attitude towards children with SEN in society and this has had an effect on attitudes towards them in school. Overall, these children are now more valued as individuals and society is increasingly more compassionate towards them. In this respect many children with SEN have a greater opportunity to participate in and contribute effectively to the life of the school.

The impact of labelling children with SEN is now better understood than earlier in the century. Without doubt, for a long period of time this led to the creation of self-fulfilling prophecies for children who felt constrained by their disabilities in school. Although the consequences of this have not been completely eliminated a more positive attitude is discernible. A more recent example relates to the statementing procedure detailed in the 1981 Education Act. This procedure, in contrast to the certification arrangements made in the 1921 Education Act, has been received in generally positive terms. In part this can be accounted for through factors relating to the overall changing attitudes prevalent in society to children with SEN.

Curriculum factors
The area of the curriculum for children with SEN has, for much of the century, been largely uncontroversial. During most of this period the curriculum for all pupils was set in an increasingly liberal and

child-centred framework. It is largely accepted that this approach with its built-in flexibility and its emphasis on individual needs and overall personal development was best suited to meet the needs of pupils with SEN.

However, the introduction of the National Curriculum in 1988 has not been helpful to many pupils with SEN. The tensions which surfaced during the initial debate on the value of full participation of pupils with SEN in the National Curriculum have now manifested themselves. The value of the concept of a 'curriculum for all' has validity and credibility by its inclusive nature. However, in practice, the nature of the National Curriculum has created considerable difficulties. The overall emphasis on the more academic subjects, as well as the approaches to assessment used, have been less than helpful to pupils with SEN. Despite the increased flexibility proposed by Dearing (DfE 1993, 1996) the curricula of mainstream schools are still determined by the National Curriculum to such an extent that providing appropriate curricula for pupils with SEN is very difficult. The debate on the value of the National Curriculum, as far as pupils with SEN are concerned, is far from over. In the period after the present moratorium on change ends in 1999, attention needs to be focused on how best to accommodate changes which will provide more satisfactory arrangements for this group of pupils.

Professional development
The area of the professional development of teachers of pupils with SEN has had a somewhat chequered history. Initially, developments in this area were limited for a variety of reasons which include a paucity of knowledge as to how best to deal with pupils with SEN and their learning difficulties and a lack of understanding of the value of such work.

As knowledge increased so did the opportunities for teachers to undertake further professional training in this area of work. For a number of years in the 1960s and 1970s, in order to aid recruitment to the SEN field, government policy actively encouraged teachers to undertake further professional development in this area, through secondments and in-service training courses. More recently, however, financial restrictions and an increasing teacher workload have created difficulties. Secondments to attend full-time courses in SEN are almost impossible to obtain and LEA and individual school sponsorship has become far less accessible. Staff who are interested in further professional development in SEN have increasingly had to finance themselves on to part-time courses, which is another current source of tension.

The call for a more competence-based approach to professional development can only increase the need for appropriate courses. The need for the development of good classroom practice with regard to pupils with SEN has increased over the last twenty years. Specifying and then working on the competences as part of training required by teachers of children with SEN should help in this regard. However, the competence-based approach has its disadvantages, particularly at post-qualification level, when the skills, understanding and knowledge needed are more complex and varied. If such moves are to be successful there is a need for a clear understanding of the roles adopted by teachers working with pupils with SEN so that the competences to be worked on are clearly identified. There must also be a flexible use of such an approach so that the roles identified are not seen as totally prescriptive.

Management issues
The analysis undertaken indicates that historically the management of SEN at all levels of its administration, particularly the strategical management of policy and planning at government and LEA levels, has been inadequate. There is evidence of conflicts over management strategies for SEN policy and provision within mainstream schools and in special schools. The main difficulties have occurred in relation to the factors relating to social, political and resourcing influences identified in the cartwheel model. It is clear that management strategies and decisions are closely connected to the social values held in a society. The influence of the Eugenicists on integration policy in the early part of the century is one example of this. Another is the effect of the development of equal opportunities legislation later in the century. The values held by society have influenced the political decisions and the legislation which is enacted by Parliament. Clearly, political decisions have a major influence on the resources and finance available to develop provision.

For much of the period of compulsory schooling the development of management strategies occurred only at an operational level within schools. Much of the available literature is concerned with applied management issues at this level. Although it would be wrong to underestimate the importance of applied management issues, it is clear that, throughout the period of compulsory education, there has been a lack of both co-ordination and consistency between developments at this level and overarching strategical management, in order to develop policy and planning at DfEE and LEA levels.

For much of the century, policy-making and planning at national and local government levels to meet the needs of pupils with SEN in mainstream schools have been virtually non-existent. A number of factors can be cited which have contributed to the difficulties which can also be related to other factors which have been identified in this book. These include: an overall lack of leadership and political will to initiate change, a lack of commitment to the education and social acceptance of those with SEN throughout society, as well as a lack of finance and other resources to facilitate developments.

A SECOND DIMENSION

In the second dimension, the seven individual factors detailed in the cartwheel model need to be considered in relation to each other. In this respect, the relationship between these factors cuts across the complete range of issues and affects the development of provision for children with SEN. This inter-relationship is not static, rather it is constantly changing. These changes are dependent on shifts in the relationship between each of them. Further, the dominant factors act as balances and checks which have either aided or impeded progress in developing SEN provision.

Within this cartwheel model the seven factors have their own hierarchy of influence and this leads to the domination of some of the factors over the others. Our analysis indicates that four of the factors have a tendency to be dominant as far as SEN policy and provision in mainstream schools are concerned. The four dominant factors are: political will, societal influences, the provision of resources and management issues.

These factors are mainly concerned with societal issues and the dominant values within these, rather than educational ones. It is the other factors: curriculum planning and professional development issues along with the question of integration, which can be placed in this second group. The factors in this latter category are the dominant factors concerned with the day-to-day practicalities of the running of the school.

The hierarchy described above is also the key determinant as to the pace and direction of policy. The most important factors in this respect are again those which operate from outside the school. The evidence presented in this book has repeatedly demonstrated the dominance of external social, economic and political factor at the expense of educational ones.

At different times during the period of compulsory schooling the forces brought to bear through conflicting interests between the seven factors have been subject to fluctuations. These fluctuations are related to changes in the overall values of society towards children with SEN. These changes have led to windows of opportunity being created to allow for progress in planning and provision for these children.

Such fluctuations have not been of seismic proportions. They have generally occurred slowly and over a considerable period of time, leading to evolutionary rather than revolutionary change. Nevertheless, such subtleties in fluctuations between the seven factors have led to points where changes which at one time would have been generally regarded as impossible or unwelcome have become acceptable or even essential.

On occasions, change has been possible as a result of interactions between a number of the factors identified in the cartwheel model. At other times this has occurred through the developments within one or two factors only. One example of the former, where change has occurred as a result of a wide range of pressures from across the seven factors, relates to the debate on integration. The pressure exerted by some of the factors for increased integration of children with SEN into mainstream schools in the early part of the century was largely ineffectual and failed to influence the recommendations of the committees of enquiry. At that time such moves were largely dismissed in a society which regarded people with disabilities as socially unacceptable, even harmful. As a result, developments in this area had to wait until other changes occurred. These included changes in the values exhibited in society to those with disabilities and shifts in attitudes to human rights as a consequence of this.

On other occasions, pressures emanating from only one or two of the seven factors have influenced the nature of changes which have occurred. One example of this is the pressures brought to bear on politicians to initiate enquiries into the needs of pupils in school with learning difficulties. Such situations occurred following the publication of the Egerton Report (1898) and before the initiation of the Warnock Committee in the early 1970s. This illustrates how changes in political will can be prompted by influences from society at large. A further example is that of parental pressures which were brought to bear to ensure the discontinuance of the certification procedure introduced in the 1921 Education Act. Similarly, parental pressure prompted the placement of a time limit on LEAs on the statementing procedure, which led to amendments in the 1993 Education Act. This example illustrates how management strategies can be influenced by pressure from social attitudes.

Policy decisions concerning children with SEN in mainstream schools are generally taken by people whose interests lie in different spheres of education or even outside it. Those working to help develop provision for children with SEN in mainstream schools in the UK start off from a position of low status and little influence. This is a situation which is not unique to this country and similar tensions can be identified in other countries in the developed world in making sound educational provision for children with SEN. There has been a coherent move in most countries in Western Europe and the USA towards the greater integration of all children into mainstream schools. Other developments which have occurred abroad are dependent on the relationship between the same seven factors as those outlined as being of importance in the UK. The differences which have occurred abroad are largely dependent on the same seven factors and their interplay.

OVERVIEW

Throughout the century, attempts which have been made to develop satisfactory practice for pupils with SEN in mainstream schools in the UK have been slow, piecemeal and often ineffectual. Recent legislation, which has been focused more directly on their needs, has attempted to improve this. The 1981 Education Act set provision in a sound philosophical framework based on contemporary thinking in the wider society. This has been complemented by the introduction of the Code of Practice which has put in place a practical framework designed to ensure effective education for pupils with SEN. The Code, however, is viewed as bureaucratic and cumbersome by many teachers. Therefore, its eventual success in bringing about constructive changes in SEN provision in mainstream schools remains to be seen.

Both the introduction of the National Curriculum (1988) and OFSTED inspections (1992) are pillars of the contemporary framework of provision for pupils with SEN. Nevertheless, both of these initiatives were introduced for the benefit of a much wider group of pupils and have focused less effectively on the overall needs of pupils with SEN. The impact of the National Curriculum in particular is debatable. Although it is arguable that a strategical policy framework is in place for children with SEN in mainstream schools it is questionable as to how effective this is. The OFSTED framework, although similar to the National Curriculum in drawing all pupils into one inspection framework, is unhelpful in its overall focus and direction with its emphasis on inspection rather than advice. The recent OFSTED report (1996), despite indicating that although many schools were making good progress in the implementation of the recommendations of the Code of Practice (1994) at an operational level, reported that much remained to be done by all those involved – teachers, governors and LEAs.

It is clear, through the findings of such reports, that the strategical planning required to make consistent provision for pupils with SEN throughout the country remains a largely unfulfilled goal. Despite the improvements noted in recent years at LEA and individual school level, provision for pupils with SEN in mainstream schools remains patchy and continues to be determined by local conditions in individual LEAs and greatly influenced by the actions of individual professionals and parents.

Evans and Lunt (1994) questioned if the DfEE (and therefore the national government) had a special needs policy at all! The evidence indicates that some links have been made between philosophical values in society about children with SEN and the curriculum provision which should be made available for them. Nevertheless, there continues to be a need to develop good practice in schools and to evaluate and monitor much more closely how this is being implemented throughout the country. There continues to be little evidence to suggest that this is a nationally co-ordinated policy or a practical way forward to developing satisfactory provision which is widely accepted by both teachers and the wider society.

Contemporary practice for pupils with SEN in mainstream schools continues to be based on little more than a series of policies and Acts of Parliament which are essentially focused on the needs and requirements of other children in their peer group. Despite the introduction of the Code of Practice, mainstream schools, when working with pupils with SEN, continue to have difficulties in reconciling this with the requirements of the National Curriculum. This situation has created its own tensions and frustrations. In this respect, the needs of pupils with SEN continue to appear to be an adjunct to the main thrust of national educational policy. Uncertainties remain as to the best approach to aid the education of pupils with SEN in order to provide them with a clear view of their role in a society where there is a decreasing number of employment opportunities for them.

For such developments to occur, the management of SEN must take into account its ethical dimension. In such a debate Howe and Miramontes (1992) discussed the administration of SEN in terms of the moral philosophy impacting on society. Their analysis indicated that there are clear ethical issues which are based on contradictions between two schools of thought. These Howe and Miramontes (1992) described as the *utilitarian approach*, and the *virtue school approach*. The utilitarian approach places its emphasis on rationality and the inclusion of all of society in the debates on policy decisions. This model acts in contradiction to the virtue school approach, with its concentration on the particular and practicability.

These contradictions can be identified in the different approaches to the management of SEN. It is the case that parents of children with SEN, their teachers and to some extent schools themselves belong to the virtue school of management of provision. The parameters of their approach are set in an essentially child-centred framework. National and local government, although acknowledging the importance of this approach, argue they have to take other factors in the wider society into account and therefore take a largely rational or utilitarian approach. They argue that such an approach is necessary in order to prioritise the overall deployment of resources and to act as a a check on the virtue school. The dichotomy between these two ethical approaches has contributed to the widespread frustrations which have been identified throughout this book.

From the point of view of parents and teachers working in mainstream schools with pupils with SEN, neither the law nor the overarching management structure can take into account every situation which will occur. However careful the planning, the individual nature of children's SEN cannot always be accounted for. The overall philosophical and ethical debate in society must not only take this into account, but address relevant issues in order to produce satisfactory policy planning and practice.

Although some lessons may have been learned as a result of experiences since the introduction of compulsory education at the end of the nineteenth century, some of the same problems which have dogged the development of SEN provision throughout this period remain today. This situation has occurred largely as a result of inconsistencies in and a lack of co-ordination of policy-making at all levels, inadequate resourcing and a lack of political will and leadership. Although it is the case that these are problems which will continue to cause difficulties for all concerned in this area of education, until these issues and the wider ethical questions which have been raised briefly here have been addressed and a greater degree of co-ordination at all levels of administration achieved, the quality of provision which is made for most pupils with SEN in mainstream schools will continue to remain unsatisfactory.

The development of sound educational policy, planning and provision for one child in five continues to be questionable. Much has been done at classroom level by interested teachers to develop provision for their pupils. There has been a personal commitment from many teachers working with pupils with SEN to professional development in the area of special education. Teachers continue to be keen to undertake courses in this area of work even when this is in their own time and they have to pay for it themselves. While demonstrating exemplary professional commitment from the teachers themselves, this is indicative of a level of commitment which needs to be matched by the wider society and political leadership.

Schools are increasingly accused of having 'a long tail' of pupils who lack the acquisition of basic skills to aid them in the post-school working environment. It is inevitable that there will be little improvement in the development of their skills until both strategical and operational management issues are co-ordinated to meet not only the needs of these pupils but also the growing aspirations for them by the wider society in an increasingly complex world. The evidence indicates that historically this has not been undertaken with any degree of satisfaction. Currently there is a framework in place through the 1981 and 1993 Education Acts, the Code of Practice and OFSTED to encourage such developments. Their effectiveness in bringing these changes about remains to be seen. Their implementation provides a framework which is essentially static in a situation where developments are inevitable. The present situation of pupils with SEN in mainstream schools remains essentially unsatisfactory from a number of different points of view. Further changes in the development of provision need to be made, taking into account the interests and values of all those concerned. These changes will continue to need to be monitored and reviewed. It is clear that the last hundred years have not produced an appropriate, efficient and systematic way of developing and sustaining progress for pupils with SEN in mainstream schools.

It has been argued in this book that this has been due to a lack of political will, inadequate resourcing, unhelpful societal attitudes, ineffective management strategies, inappropriate curricula, inadequate training opportunities and disagreements over the extent of integration which is possible in the mainstream school. Although there are some hopeful aspects, each of these factors continues to be problematic. It is considered that long-lasting progress in the development of effective provision for pupils with SEN in mainstream schools will not be forthcoming unless difficulties in all of the seven areas are addressed.

Bibliography

Adams, F. (ed) (1986) *Special Education*. Harlow, Longman.

Ainscow, M. and Tweddle, D. A. (1979) *Preventing Classroom Failure*. Chichester, Willey.

Allen (1994) in Riddell, S. and Brown, S. *Special Educational Needs Policy in the 1990s: Warnock in the Market Place*. London, Routledge.

Archer, M. (1993) 'Set for Scrutiny', *Managing School Today*, February 1993 4–6.

Armstrong, D. and Galloway, D. (1994) 'Special Educational Needs and Problem Behaviour: Making Policy in the Classroom' in Riddell, S. and Brown, S. *Special Educational Needs Policy in the 1990s: Warnock in the Market Place*. London, Routledge.

Arnold, M. (1883) in Booth, T. *Origins*. Special Needs in Education, Open University Course E241 (9), Milton Keynes, Open University Press (1982).

Association of Metropolitan Authorities (Morris, R. *et al* 1993) *Education Act '93: A Critical Guide*. London, AMA.

Audit Commission and HMI (1992a) *Getting in on the Act: Provision for Pupils with SEN: The National Picture*. London, HMSO.

Audit Commission and HMI (1992b) *Getting the Act Together*. London, HMSO.

Baker, K. (1988) in the *Times Educational Supplement*, 8 January.

Banks, O. and Findlayson, D. (1984) *Success and Failure in the Secondary School*. London, Methuen.

Bardis, P. (1993) 'Integration of Children with Special Needs in Rural Greece' in O'Hanlon, C. *Integration in Europe*. London, David Fulton.

Baron, P. A. (1938) *Backwardness in Schools*. London, Blackie.

Barthorpe, T. and Visser, J. (1992) *Differentiation. Your Responsibility*. Stafford, NASEN.

Barton, L. and Tomlinson, S. (eds) (1984) *Special Education and Social Interest*. London, Croom Helm.

Batty, P. *et al* (1987) 'Changing the Curriculum at Peers', *British Journal of Special Education* 14 (3).

Bell, G., Stakes, J. R. and Taylor, G. (1994) *Action Research, Special Needs and School Development*. London, David Fulton.

Bell, J. (1987) *Doing Your Research Project. A Guide for First Time Researchers in Education and Social Science*. Milton Keynes, Open University Press.

Bell, J., Bush, T., Fox, A., Goodey, J. and Goulding, S. (eds) (1984) *Conducting Small Scale Investigations in Educational Management*. London, Paul Chapman.

Bell, P. (1970) *Basic Teaching for Slow Learners*. London, Miller.

Benger, K. (1971) in Rogers, T. J. G. (ed) *School for the Community*. London, Routledge and Keegan Paul.

Bennis, W. G., Benne, K. D. and Chin, R. (eds) (1967) *The Planning of Change*. New York, Reinhart and Winston.

Berliner, W. (1993) 'Needs are not being met', in *The Guardian Educational*, June 8.

Bernstein, L. (1968) *Management Development*. London, Business Books.

Birch, L. B. (1948) 'The remedial treatment of reading disability', *Educational Review* (1) 107–118.

Birley, D. (1972) *Planning and Education*. London, Routledge and Keegan Paul.

Blane, D. C. and Englehardt, V. (1984) 'Maths Clinics: the Implementation for children with Learning Difficulties', *Remedial Education* 19 (3) 107–112.

Blenkin, G. M., Edwards, G. and Kelly, A. V. (1992) *Change and the Curriculum*. London, Paul Chapman.

Blishen, E. (1955) *Roaring Boys*. London, Thames and Hudson.

Blishen, E. Reported by Segal, S. S. (1967) *Teachers' World*, 3 May.

Board of Education (1888) Cross Commission. *Board of Education*. London, HMSO.

Board of Education (1927) *The Education of the Adolescent: Report of Consultative Committee*. Hadow, W. H. London, HMSO.

Board of Education (1937) *The Education of Backward Children*. Pamphlet 112. London, HMSO.

Board of Education (1938) *Report of the Consultative Committee on Secondary Education with Special Reference to grammar schools and technical high schools*. London, HMSO.

Bookbinder, G. (1982) *The 1981 Education Act: a Discordant View*. Unpublished Paper.

Booth, T. and Potts, P. (eds) (1983) *Integrating Special Education*. Oxford, Blackwell.

Booth, T., Potts, P. and Swann, W. (eds) (1987) *Preventing Difficulties in Learning: Curricula for All*. Oxford, Basil Blackwell.

Booth, T. (1992) 'Integration, disability and commitment' in Booth, T., Swann, W., Masterson, M. and Potts, P. (eds) *Policies for Diversity in Education*. London, Routledge.

Booth, T. and Swann, W. (1982) *Special Needs in Education, An Alternative System: A Special Imagination*. Open University Course E241 (16), Milton Keynes, Open University Press.

Booth, T. and Statham, J. (1982) *The Nature of Special Education*. London, Croom Helm.

Booth, T. (1982a) *Special Needs in Education, Eradicating Handicap*. Open University Course E241 (14), Milton Keynes, Open University Press.

Booth, T. (1982b) *Special Needs in Education, Origins*. Open University Course E241 (9), Milton Keynes, Open University Press.

Booth, T. (1982c) *Special Needs in Education: National Perspectives*. Open University Course E241 (10), Milton Keynes, Open University Press.

Booth, T. (1981) in Swann, W. (1981) *The Practice of Special Education*. Oxford, Blackwell.

Borg, W. R. (1976) *Ability Groups in Public Schools*. Madison Wisc, Dernbar Education Research Services.

Bowers, T. (1985) *Managing Special Needs*. Milton Keynes, Open University Press.

Bowie, S. and Robertson, J. (1985) 'Co-operation in a Mixed Ability Role at Secondary Level', *Remedial Education* 20 (1) 129–134.

Bowman, I. (1981) in Swann, W. (1981) *The Practice of Special Education*. Oxford, Blackwell.

Bradley, C. and Roaf, C. (1995) 'Meeting Special Educational Needs in the Secondary School: a team approach' in *Support for Learning* 10 (ii) 93–99.

Brennan, W. K. (Chairman) (1979) *Curricular Needs of Slow Learners. Schools Council Working Party 63*. London, Evans/School Council.

Brennan, W. K. (1985) *Curriculum for Special Needs*. Milton Keynes, Open University Press.

Brennan, W. K. (1973) The curricular needs of Slow learning pupils: Some Considerations. *Special Education Forward Trends*. 12 (2) 59–62.

Brennan, W. K. (1974) *Shaping the Education of Slow Learners*. London, Routledge and Keegan Paul.

Brennan, W. K. (1982) *Special Education in Mainstream Schools: the Search for Quality*. Stafford, NCSE.

Buddenhagen, R. G. (1967) 'Towards a Better Understanding', *Mental Retardation* 5 (2) 22–37.

Bullock, A. (Chairman) (1975) *A Language for Life*. London, HMSO.

Burden, R. (1988) 'To Integrate or not to Integrate, that is the Question' in Gurney, P. (ed) *Special Education in the Ordinary School. Perspectives* 15, Exeter, School of Education, the University of Exeter.

Burnes, B. (1992) *Managing Change: A Strategic Approach to Organisational Development*. London, Pitman.

Burnes, T. and Stalker, G. M. (1961) *The Management of Innovation*. London, Tavistock.

Burt, C. (1921) *Mental and Scholastic Tests*. London, P S King and Son.

Burt, C. (1937) *The Backward Child*. London, Hodder and Stoughton.

Burt, C. (1935) *The Sub Normal Mind*. Oxford, Oxford University Press.

Bushell, R. S. (1979) 'The Warnock Report and Section 10 of the 1976 Education Act, Integration or Segregation', *Remedial Education* 14 (1) 27–30.

Butler, V. G. (1985) *Organisation and Management*. London, Prentice Hall.

Butt, N. (1986) 'Implementing the Whole School Approach at Secondary Level', *Support for Learning* 1 (4) 10–15.

Calvocoressi, P. (1978) *The British Experience (1945–75)*. London, Bodley Head.

Cameron, R. J. (1981) 'Curriculum Development 1: Classifying and Planning Curriculum Objectives', *Remedial Education* 16 (4) 163–171.

Capron, A. C., Simon, A. and Ward, L. O. (1980a) 'Principles for the Integration of Remedial Pupils in a Comprehensive School', *Remedial Education* 18 (2) 75–80.

Capron, A. C., Simon, A. and Ward, L. O. (1980b) 'The Academic and Social Implications of Integrating First Year Remedial Secondary Pupils', *Remedial Education* 15 (4) 164–169.

Capron, A. C. (1978) *Integration v Segregation for Remedial Pupils in their first year at Secondary School*. Unpublished M Phil. Thesis, University of Wales.

Carlberg, C. and Kavale, K. (1990) 'The efficacy of special versus regular class placement for exceptional children: A meta analysis', *Journal of Special Education* 14 (7) 295–309.

Carpenter, B. and Bovair, K. (1990) 'The silly season for training', *British Journal of Special Education* 17 (4) 136.

Cave, R. C. and Maddison, M. (1978) 'A Survey of Recent Research in Special Education', *Special Education* 1 (4).

Cave, R. C. (1968) *All their Futures*. London, Penguin.

Ceisla, M. J. (1979) 'Geography for Slow Learners in the Secondary School', *Remedial Education* 14 (2).

Chapman, J. V. (1969) *Your Secondary Modern Schools*. London, College of Preceptors.

Chapman, J. W. (1988) 'Special education in the least restrictive environment: mainstreaming or maindumping', *Australia and New Zealand Journal of Developmental Disabilities* 14 (2) 123–134.

Charity Organisation Society (1893) *The Feeble Minded Child and Adult: A Report on an Investigation of the Physical and Mental Conditions of 50,000 School Children*. London, Swann Sonnenschien.

Cheshire Education Committee (1985) *Provision for Special Educational Needs in the Secondary School*. Unpublished Internal Document.

Cheshire Education Committee (1963) *The Education of Dull Children at the Secondary Stage*. London, University of London Press.

Cheshire Education Committee (1958) *The Secondary Modern School*.

London, University of London Press.

Chuter Ede, J. (1944) 'Parliamentary Debates', *Hansard* 389, Col 703, March.

Clarke, A. M. and Clarke, A. D. B. (eds) (1965) *Mental Deficiency, The Changing Outlook*. London, Methuen.

Clark, C., Dyson, A. and Millward, A. (eds) (1995) *Towards Inclusive Schools?* London, David Fulton.

Clegg, A. and Mason, B. (1968) *Children in Distress*. London, Penguin.

Clench, H. and Tyler, B. (1986) 'The WSIHE–Croydon Scheme: a model for the future', *British Journal of In Service Education* 13 (1) 26–30.

Cleugh, M. F. (1961) *Teaching Slow learners in the Secondary School*. London, Methuen.

Clunies-Ross, L. and Wilmhurst, S. (1983) *The Right Balance. Provision for the Slow Learner in Secondary Schools*. Windsor, NFER.

Clunies-Ross, L. (1984a) 'In-Service Training for Teaching Slow Learners', *Remedial Education* 19 (1) 154–156.

Clunies-Ross, L. (1984b) 'Supporting the Mainstream Teacher', *Special Education Forward Trends* 11 (3) 9–11.

Cocker, C. (1995) 'Special Needs in the Infant School' in *Support for Learning* 10 (ii) 75–82.

Cohen, A. and Cohen, L. (eds) (1986) *Special Educational Needs in the Ordinary School: a source-book for Teachers*. London, PCP.

Cole, E. (1989) *Apart or A part?* Milton Keynes, Open University Press.

Cole, T. (1990) 'The History of Special Education: Social Control or Humanitarian Process', *British Journal of Special Education* 17 (3) 101–107.

Collins, J. E. (1965) 'The Remedial Hoax', *Remedial Education* 1 (4) 10–12.

Collins, J. E. (1961) *The Effects of Remedial Education*. Birmingham, University of Birmingham Institute of Education.

Coopers and Lybrand (1997) as yet unpublished document.

Cope, C. and Anderson, E. (1977) *Special Units in Ordinary Schools*. London, London University Institute of Education.

Cornell, P. in Watts, J. (1974) *The Countsthorpe Experience*. London, Unwin.

Corwen, R. G. (1981) 'Patterns of Organisational Control and Teacher Militancy: Theoretical Continuities of the Idea of Loose Coupling', *Research in the Sociology of Education* (2) 261–291.

Council for National Academic Awards (1991) 'Review of Special Educational Needs', *Initial and In Service Teacher Education Courses*. London, CNAA.

Cox, C. B. and Dyson, A. E. (eds) (1971) *The Black Papers on Education (1969, 1970)*. London, Davis-Poynter.

Cox, B. (1985) *The Laws of Special Educational Needs, A Guide to the*

Education Act 1981. London, Croom Helm.

Craft, M., Raynor, J. and Cohen, L. (1967) *Linking Home and School*. London, Longman.

Cripps, C. (1979) 'Spelling a Safe Account', *Remedial Education* 14 (3) 146–149.

Croll, P. and Moses, D. (1985) *One in Five. An Assessment and Incidence of Special Educational Needs*. London, Routledge and Keegan Paul.

Cruickshank, W. M. (1974) 'The false hope of integration', *The Slow Learning Child* 21 (2) 67–83.

Cubberley, E. P. (1916) *Public School Administration*. Boston, Houghton Miffin.

Cummings, T. G. and Huse, E.F. (1989) *Organisational Development and Change*. St Paul, Minnesota, West.

Curry, S. A. and Hatlen, P. H. (1988) 'Meeting the unique educational needs of visually impaired pupils through appropriate placement', *Journal of Visual Impairment and Blindness* 82 (10) 417–424.

Danby, J. and Cullen, C. 'Integration and mainstreaming: a review of the efficacy of mainstreaming and integration for mentally handicapped pupils', *Educational Psychology* 8 (3) 177–195.

Daniels, E. A. (1984) 'Suggested Model of Remedial Provision in a Comprehensive School', *Remedial Education* 19 (2) 78–82.

Daniels, H., Porter, J. and Sandow, S. (1988) 'New issues in in service education', *British Journal of Special Education* 15 (3) 127–129.

Davie, R. (1976) *Children and Families with Special Needs*. Inaugural Lecture of Professor of Education, University of Wales.

Davie, R. in Pike, N. (1996) 'Expenditure fear over special help', *Times Educational Supplement*, 29 November, p 3.

Davies, J. D. and Davies, P. (1988) 'Developing credibility as a support teacher', *Support for Learning* 3 (1) 12–15.

Davis, W. J. K. (1978) *Implementing Individualised Learning*. London, Council for Educational Technology.

Dean, J. (1989) *Special Needs in the Secondary School: The Whole School Approach*. London, Routledge.

Dearden, R. F., Hirst, P. H. and Peters, R. S. (eds) (1975) *A Critique of Current Educational Aims*. London, Routledge and Keegan Paul.

Dearing, R. (1994) *The National Curriculum and its Assessment. A Final Report*. London, Schools Curriculum and Assessment Authority.

Dearing, R. (1996) *Review of Qualifications for 16-19 Year Olds. Summary Report*. London, SCAA.

Deno, E. (1970) 'Special education as developmental capital', *Exceptional Children* 37 229–237.

Department for Education (1994) *Code of Practice on the Identification and Assessment of Special Educational Needs*. London, Central Office of Information.

Department for Education (1990) *Education (National Curriculum)*

(Assessment) Targets Number 2 Order. London, HMSO.

Department for Education (1992) *Exclusions: A Discussion Paper.* London, Department for Education.

Department for Education (1993) *Local Management of Schools. The Future Framework* (Consultation Document). London, Department for Education.

Department for Education (1992) *Special Needs and the National Curriculum.* London, HMSO.

Department of Education and Science (Welsh Office) (1978) *Special Educational Needs DES/Welsh Office Consultative Document.* HMSO, Cardiff.

Department of Education and Science (1986) *A Report by HMI. A Survey of Lower Attainers Programmes (LAPPs)* London, HMSO.

Department of Education and Science (1980) *A View of the Curriculum.* (HMI Series, Education Matters (2)). London, HMSO.

Department of Education and Science (1979) *Aspects of Secondary Education in Schools in England and Wales. A Survey by HMI.* London, HMSO.

Department of Education and Science (1992) *Choice and Diversity, A New Framework for Schools.* White Paper on Education. London, HMSO.

Department of Education and Science (1965) *Circular 10/65.* London, HMSO.

Department of Education and Science (1988) *Secondary Schools; an Appraisal by HMIs A report Based on Inspections in England and Wales (1982–1986).* London, DES.

Department of Education and Science (1984) *Slow Learning and Less Successful Pupils in Secondary Schools. Evidence from Some HMI Visits.* London, DES.

Department of Education and Science (1989) *Statistics of Education. Schools 1988.* Circular 24/89. London, HMSO.

Department of Education and Science (1959) *The Handicapped Pupil and Special School Regulations.* London, HMSO.

Department of Education (1971) *Slow Learners in Secondary School.* Educational Survey 15. London, HMSO.

Department of Education and Science (1989) Circular 22/89. *Assessments and Statements of Special Educational Needs: Procedures within the Education, Health and Social Service.* London, DES.

Department for Education (1994) *The Organisation of Special Educational Provision.* Circular 6/94. London, DfE.

Department for Education and Employment (1996) *Special Educational Needs in England.* London, DfEE.

Dessant, T. (1989) 'To Statement or not to Statement?' (Editorial), *British Journal of Special Education* 16 (1) 5.

Detraux, J. J. and Dens, A. (1992) 'Special Education in Belgium', *European Journal of Special Needs Education* 7 (1) 63–79.

Dobbins, D. A. (1985) 'How teachers can use the Diagnostic Remedial Method to improve Attainment in Reading: an example', *Remedial Education* 20 (2) 79–85.

Douglas, J. B. W., Ross, J. M. and Simpson, H. R. (1971) *All our Future.* London, Panther.

Douglas, J. B. W. (1964) *The Home and the School.* London, Panther.

Drucker, P. F. (1974) *Management: Tasks, Responsibilities, Practices.* London, Harper and Row.

Dugdale, R. L. (1977) *The Juves, a study in Crime, Paupers, Disease and Heredity.* New York, Pitman.

Duncan, J. (1942) *The Education of the Ordinary Child.* London, Nelson.

Dunn, L. M. (1968) 'Special education for the mildly retarded: Is much of it justified?', *Exceptional Children* (5) 5–22.

Dust, K. (1988) 'The Diploma courses' in Hegarty, S. and Moses, D. (eds) *Developing Expertise: Inset for Special Educational Needs.* Windsor, NFER-Nelson.

Dyer, C. (1988) 'What Support? An Evaluation of the Term', *Support for Learning* 3 (1) 79–85.

Dyson, A. (1990) 'Effective learning Consultancy: A future role for special needs coordinators?', *Support for Learning* 5 (3) 116–127.

Dyson, A. (1991) 'It's not What You Do It's the Way That You Do It', *Remedial Education* 16 (3).

Dyson, A. (1992) *Special needs in Mainstream Schools: Emerging practice.* A First Report of the IMP Project. Newcastle, University of Newcastle upon Tyne.

Dyson, A. and Gains, C. (1995) 'The Role of the Special Needs Coordinator: Poisoned Chalice or Crock of Gold', *Support for Learning* 10 (2).

Edwards, J. B. (1973) 'Remedial Education post Warnock, Implementation or revival?', *Remedial Education* 8 (1) 9–14.

Evans, J. and Lunt, J. (1994) 'Special Educational Provision After LMS', *British Journal of Special Education* 20 (2).

Evans, R. (1982) in Hinson, M. and Hughes, M. *Planning Effective Progress.* Amersham, Hulton/NARE.

Everard, K. B. (1984) *Management in Comprehensive Schools.* York, University of York Centre for the Study of Comprehensive Schools.

Fergueson, N. and Adams, M. (1982) 'Assessing the Advantages of Team Teaching in Remedial Education, the Remedial teacher's Role', *Remedial Education* 17 (1) 24–31.

Ferneaux, B. (1976) *The Special Child.* London, Penguin.

Fish, J. (1985) *Special Education. The Way Ahead.* Milton Keynes, Open University Press.

Fish, J. and Evans J. (1995) *Managing Special Education.* Milton Keynes, Open University Press.

Fisher, G. (1977) 'Integration at Pringle School', *Special Education*

Forward Trends 4 (1) 8–11.

Floud, J. E., Halsey, A. H. and Martin, F. M. (1956) *Social Class and Educational Opportunity.* London, Heinemann.

Ford, J. (1982) *Special Education and Social Control.* London, Routledge and Keegan Paul.

Fox, E. (1918) 'The Mental Deficiency Act and its Administration', *Eugenics Review* (10) 1– 17.

Fraser, E. D. (1982) *Home Environment and the School.* London, London University Press.

French, W. L. and Bell, C. H. (1984) *Organization Development.* Eaglewood Cliffs, New Jersey, Prentice Hall.

Furnham, A. and Gibbs, M. (1884) 'School Children's Attitudes towards the Handicapped', *Journal of Adolescence.*

Gains, C. W. (1980) 'Remedial Education in the 1980s', *Remedial Education* 15 (1) 5–10.

Gains, C. and McNicholas, J. (1979) *Guidelines for the Future.* London, Longman.

Gallagher, J. (1973) 'Current Trends in Special Education in the United States', *International Review of Education* 20 (3).

Galton, F. (1909) *The Problems of the Feeble Minded.* London, P S King.

Garner, P. (1995) 'Sense or Nonsense? Dilemmas in the SEN Code of Practice', *Support for Learning* 10 (i) 3–7.

Garner, P. (1996) *A special Education? The experiences of newly qualified teachers during initial teacher training.* Abingdon, Carfax Publishing Company.

Garner, P. (1996) 'Students' views on special educational needs courses in Initial Teacher Education', *British Journal of Special Education* 24 (4) 176–179.

Garner, A. and Lipsky, D. K. (1989) 'New conceptualizations for special education', *European Journal of Special Needs Education* 4 (1) 16–21.

Garnet, J. (1976) *Special Education Forward Trends* 3 (1).

Giles, C. and Dunlop, S. (1986) 'Changing Directions at Tile Hill Wood', *British Journal of Special Education* 13 (3) 120–123.

Gipps, C., Gross, H. and Goldstein, H. (1987) *Warnock's Eighteen Percent. Children with Special needs in the Primary School.* Lewes, Falmer.

Gleidman, J. and Roth, W. (1981) in Swann, W. (ed) *The Practice of Special Education.* Milton Keynes, Blackwell's Open University Press.

Goacher, B., Evans, J., Welton, J., Weddell, K. and Glaser, A. (1986) *The 1981 Education Act: policy and provision for Special Educational Needs. A report for the DES.* London, London University Institute of Education.

Goacher, B., Evans, J., Welton, J. and Welddell, K. (1988) *Policy and Provision for Special Educational Needs: Implementing the 1981 Education Act.* London, Cassell.

Goddard, H. H. (1912) *The Kallikak Family*. New York, Macmillan.

Goodson, I. F. (1987) *School Subjects and Curriculum Change*. London, Falmer Press.

Gordon, M. (1983) 'Because they're better than us. Planning for Failure in the Secondary School', *Remedial Education* 18 (4) 174–177.

Gordon, N. and Wilson, N. (1979) 'Helping the Inadequate – a Flexible Approach', *Remedial Education* 14 (3).

Gordon, V. (1992) *Your primary School*. Stafford, National Association of Remedial Education.

Gottlieb, J. (1987) 'Mainstreaming: Fulfilling the promise?', *American Journal of Mental Deficiency* 86 (2) 115–126.

Graham, D. and Tytler D. (1993) *A lesson for us all. The Making of the National Curriculum*. London, Routledge.

Green, L. (1968) *Parents and Teachers, Partners or Rivals?* London, George Allen and Unwin.

Gulliford, R. (1969) *Backwardness and Educational Failure*. Slough, NFER.

Gulliford, R. and Upton, G. (1991) *Special Educational Needs*. London, Routledge.

Haigh, G. (ed) (1977) *On Our Side*. London, Temple Smith.

Hanko, G. (1985) *Special Needs in Ordinary Classrooms*. Oxford, Blackwell.

Hansard 14 ii 44. Chuter Ede: Column 1139 (1944).

Hansard 6 vi 93. Lady Blatch: Column 1268–1270 (1993).

Hansard 29 iv (1993).

Hargreaves, D. H. (1967) *Social Relations in the Secondary School*. London, Routledge and Keegan Paul.

Hargreaves, D. H. (1972) *Interpersonal Relations and Education*. London, Routledge and Keegan Paul.

Hargreaves, D. H. (1983) *The Challenge for the Comprehensives*. London, Routledge and Keegan Paul.

Harland, J. and Weston, P. (1987) 'LAPP: Joseph's Coat of Many Colours', *British Journal of Special Education* 14 (4) 150–152.

Harnett, P. (1986) 'A new approach to INSET for special needs', *British Journal of In-Service Education* 13 (1) 23–26.

Harrison, C. (1980) *Readability in the Classroom*. Cambridge, Cambridge University Press.

Hart, S. (1986) 'Evaluating Support Teaching', *Gnosis* (9) 26.

Hartley, J. (1978) *Designing Instructional Text*. London, Kegan Pope.

Harvey, J. (1995) 'The Role of the SEN Co-ordinator at Marton Grove Primary School', *Support for Learning* 10 (2) 79–82.

Havelock, R. G. (1971) 'The Utilisation of Educational Research and Development', *British Journal of Educational Technology* 2 (2) 84–97.

Haviland, J. (ed) (1988) *Take Care Mr Baker*. London, Fourth Estate.

Haywood, R. and Wooten, M. (1988) 'The Gateshead LAPP; Prevocational Education in a Cold Climate', *Forum* 28 (3).

Hegarty, S. and Moses, D. (eds) (1988) *Developing Expertise: Inset for Special Educational Needs*. Windsor, NFER Nelson.

Hegarty, S. and Pocklington, K. (with Lucas, D.) (1982) *Integration in Action, Case Studies in the Integration of Pupils with Special Needs*. Windsor, NFER/Nelson.

Hegarty, S. and Pocklington, K. (with Lucas, D.) (1982) *Educating pupils with SEN in the Ordinary School*. Windsor, NFER/Nelson.

Hegarty, S. (1981) 'Meeting Special Educational Needs in the Ordinary School', *Educational Research* 24 (3).

Hegarty, S. (1987) *Meeting Special Needs in Ordinary Schools: An Overview*. London, Cassell.

Helgeland, I. (1992) 'Special Education in Norway', *European Journal of Special Needs Education* 7 (2) 169–183.

Hemming, J. (1981) *The Betrayal of Youth. Secondary Education Must be Changed*. London, Maryon Boyers.

Henderson, D. (1991) 'Swimming in the mainstream', *Times Educational Supplement* October 25, p 18.

Henderson, R. A. (1995) 'Worldwide school reform movements and students with disabilities', *British Journal of Special Education* 22 (4) 148–151.

Hennessy, P. (1992) *Never Again. Britain (1945–1951)*. London, Cape.

Herzberg, F. (1966) *Work and the Nature of Man*. New York, Staples Press.

Hill, M. E. (1939) *The Education of Backward Children*. London, Harrap.

Hinson, M. (1985) in Smith, C. J. (ed) (1985) *New Directions in Remedial Education*. Lewis, Falmer.

Hinson, M. and Hughes, M. (1982) *Planning Effective Progress*. Amersham, Hulton/NARE.

Hirst, P. H. and Peters, R. S. (1970) *The Logic of Education*. London, Routledge and Keegan Paul.

HMI (1982) *Provision for Primary Pupils with Statements of Special Educational Needs*. London, HMSO.

HMI (1989) *A Survey of Pupils with SEN in Ordinary Schools*. London, DES.

HMSO (1899) *Education Act (1899)*. London, HMSO.

HMSO (1929) *Board of Education and Board of Control. Report of the Joint Departmental Committee on Mental Deficiency*. London, HMSO.

HMSO (19) *Education (School Information Regulations)*. London, HMSO.

HMSO (1893) *Education Act (1893)*. London, HMSO.

HMSO (1976) *Education Act (1976)*. London, HMSO.

HMSO (1980) *Education Act (1980)*. London, HMSO.

HMSO (1944) *Education Act (1944)*. London, HMSO.

HMSO (1943) (Green Paper) *Education After the War*. London, HMSO.

HMSO (1964) *Slow Learners at School*. Pamphlet No 46. London, HMSO.

HMSO (1989) *The Education (National Curriculum) Attainment Targets and Programmes of Study in Science and Maths*. London, HMSO.

HMSO (1981) *The Education Act (1981)*. London, HMSO.

HMSO (1921) *The Education Act (1921)*. London, HMSO.

HMSO (1889) *The Report of The Royal Commission on the Blind, Deaf and Dumb etc. The Egerton Report*. London, HMSO.

HMSO (1907) *The Royal Commission on the Care and Control of the Feeble Minded*. London, HMSO.

HMSO (1893) *The Committee on Defective and Epileptic children. The Sharpe Committee*. London, HMSO.

Hockley, L. (1988) 'On Being a Support Teacher', *British Journal of Special Education* 12 (1) 156–160.

Hodgson, A., Clunies-Ross, L. and Hegarty, S. (1989) *Learning Together. Teaching Pupils with Special Educational Needs in Ordinary Schools*. Windsor, NFER.

Holly, P. (1987) *The Dilemma of the Low Attainer*. London, FEU.

Holt, J. (1964) *How Children Learn*. London, Penguin.

Hopkins, D. (1985) *A Teacher's Guide to Classroom Research*. Buckingham, Open University Press.

Hornby, G. (1990) 'A Modular Approach to Training', *British Journal of Special Education* 17 (4) 156–160.

Hornby, G. (1992) 'Integration of children with special educational needs: Is it time for a policy review?', *British Journal of Special Education* 17 (4) 156–160.

Hornby, G. (1995) 'The Code of Practice: boon or burden?', *British Journal of Special Education* 22 (3) 116–119.

Hornby, G. (1995b) *Working with Parents of Childen with Special Needs*. London, Cassell.

Hornby, G., Taylor, G. and Davis, G. (1995) *Special Educational Needs Co-ordinator's Handbook: Guidelines for Implementing the Code of Practice*. London, Routledge.

Hornby, G., Wickham, P. and Zielinski, A. (1991) 'Establishing competences for training teachers of children with special educational needs', *European Journal of Special Needs Education* 6 (1) 30–36.

House, E. R. (1974) *The Politics of Educational Innovation*. Berkeley Ca, McCrutchan Publishing Corporation.

Howe, K.R. and Miramontes, O. B. (1992) *The Ethics of Special Education*. New York, Teacher's College Press.

Hughes, M., Ribbens, P. and Thomas, H. (1987) *Managing Education: The System and the Institution*. London, Cassell.

Humberside County Council (1988) *Mainstreaming Approaches to meeting Special Educational needs: Policy and Guidelines for Schools and Colleges*. Beverley, Humberside County Council.

Humphreys, S. and Gordon, P. (1992) *Out of Sight. The Experience of Disability 1900–1950*. Plymouth, Northcote House.

Hurt, J. S. (1988) *Outside the Mainstream*. London, Batsford.

Illich, I. (1971) *Deschooling Society*. London, Calder Boyes.

Ingram, A. S. (1958) *Elementary Education at the Time of Payment by Results*. London, Longman.

Ingram, C. P. (1936) *Educating the Slow Learning Child*. London, Harrap.

Inskeep, A. D. (1930) *Teaching Dull and Retarded Children*. New York, MacMillan.

Jackson, B. and Marsden, D. (1962) *Education and the Working class*. London, Routledge and Keegan Paul.

Jackson, S. (1966) *Special education in England and Wales*. Oxford, Oxford University Press.

Jane Brown (pseudonym) (June 1993) 'Caught within a Climate of Fear', *Guardian Educational*.

Johnson, D. W. and Johnson, R. T. (1987) *Learning Together and Alone* (2nd edition). Englewood Cliffs NJ, Prentice Hall.

Johnson, G. and Scholes, K. (1993) *Exploring Corporate Strategy* (3rd edition). Prentice Hall.

Jones, E. and Berrick, S. (1980) 'Adapting a Resourceful Approach', *Special Education Forward Trends* 7 (1) 11–14.

Jones, H. G. in Mittler, P. (ed) (1970) *The Psychological Approach to Physical and Mental Handicap*. London, Methuen.

Jones, J. (1980) 'A Structured Programme for Individual Spelling Needs', *Remedial Education* 15 (4) 194–196.

Jones, N. (1990) *Special Educational Needs Review* (3). Lewis, Falmer Press.

Jones, N. J. and Southgate, T. (1983) 'Integrating the Ormerod Children', *Special Education Forward Trends* 10 (2).

Jones, N. J. and Southgate, T. (1989) *The Management of Special Needs in Ordinary Schools*. London, Routledge.

Jones Davies, C. (ed) (1975) *The Slow Learner in the Secondary School: principles and practice for organisations*. London, Ward Lock.

Jordan, R. and Powell, S. (1995) 'Skills without understanding: a critique of a competency based model of teacher education in relation to special needs', *British Journal of Special Education* 22 (3) 120–124.

Kane, A. (1996) 'The SEN Code of Practice: A fraud designed to fail or a receipt for disruption?', *The Career Teacher*, January.

Kauffman, J. M. and Hallahan, D. P. (eds) *The Illusion of Full Inclusion: A comprehensive Critique of a Current Special Education Bandwaggon*. Austin TX, Pro Ed.

Kelly, A. V. (1982) *The Curriculum: Theory and Practice*. London, Harper Row.

Kelly, D. (1981) 'Withdrawal for Help in Secondary School', *Remedial Education* 16 (2) 67–71.

Kennedy Fraser, D. (1932) *Education and the Backward Child.* London, London University Press.

Kirk, S. A. (1964) 'Research in Education' in Stevens, H. A. and Heber, R. (eds) *Mental Retardation.* Chicago, University of Chicago Press.

Kirkaldy, B. (1990) 'Special Education: Towards a question of civil rights', *The Psychologist* 3 (10) 466–467.

Kogan, M. (1972) *The Politics of Educational Change.* London, Fontana.

Kyle, C. and Davies, K. (1991) 'Attitudes of Mainstream Pupils towards Mental Retardation. A pilot study in a Leeds secondary school', *British Journal of Special Education* 18 (3).

Lacey, C. (1970) *Hightown Grammar.* Manchester, Manchester University Press.

Lacey, P. (1995) 'In the Front Line: Special educational needs co-ordinators and Liaison' in *Support for Learning* 10 (ii) 57–62.

Lavers, P., Pickup, N. and Thompson, M. (1986) 'Factors to be Considered in Implementing an in-class Support System within Secondary Schools', *Support for Learning* 1 (3) 32–35.

Lawrence, P. R. and Lorsch, J. W. (1967) *Organisation and Environment.* Boston, Harvard Business School.

Lawson, D. and Silver, H. (1973) *A History of Education in England and Wales.* London, Methuen.

Leach, D. J. and Raybould, E. C. (1977) *Learning and Behavioural Difficulties in School.* London, Open Books.

Lee, T. (1992) 'Finding Simple Answers to Complex Questions Funding Special Needs under LMS', in Wallace, G. *Local Management of Schools. Research and Experience, BERA Dialogues No 6.* Clevedon, Multilingual Matters.

Lefevre, P. (1989) 'Fishing for Funds', *Times Educational Supplement*, 2 June.

Lemin, K. (1958) 'Group Decisions and Social Change' in Swanson, G. E., Newcomb, T. M. and Hartley, E. L. (eds) *Readings in Social Psychology.*

Leonard, M. (1988) *The Education Act (1988): A Tactical Guide for Schools.* Oxford, Blackwell.

Lerner, J. W. (1973) *Children with Learning Difficulties.* London, Houghton Miffen.

Lewis, A. (1991) *Primary Special Needs and the National Curriculum.* London, Routledge.

Lewis, A., Neill S. R. S. J. and Campbell R. J. (1996) *The Implementation of the Code of Practice in Primary and Secondary Schools.* London, National Union of Teachers.

Lewis, G. (1984) 'A Supportive Role at Secondary Level', *Remedial Education* 19 (1) 7–12.

Liell, P. 'Special Pleading', *Times Educational Supplement*, October 25, p 18.

Lloyd, J. W. and Gambatese, C. (1991) 'Reforming the Relationship between Regular and Special Education: Background Issues' in Lloyd, J. W., Singh, N. N. and Repp, A. C. (eds) *The Regular Education Initative: alternative perspectives on concepts, issues and models*. Sycamore IL, Sycamore Publishing Company.

Lindsey, G. (1989) Evaluating Integration *Educational Psychology in practice* 5 (1) 7–16.

London County Council (1937) *Report of the Committee of inspectors on Backwardness in Elementary Schools.*. London, London County Council.

Lowdon, G. (1984) 'Integrating Slow Learners in Wales', *Special Education Forward Trends* 11 (4) 25–26.

Lukes, J. in Swann, W. (1981) *The Practice of Special Education*. Oxford, Blackwell.

Lumsden, J. (1968) 'Special Education for the Handicapped', *Teacher of the Blind* 56 (4).

Lunt, I. and Evans, J. (1994) *Allocating Resources for Special Educational Needs Provision*. Stafford, NASEN.

Lunt, I. and Evans, J. (1990) 'Purse Strings', *Times Educational Supplement*, 28 ix 1990 p PR8.

Lunt, I. and Evans, J. (1991) *Special Educational Needs under LMS*. London, Institute of Education, University of London.

Madden, N. A. and Slavin, R. E. 'Maintaining students with mild handicaps: Academic and social outcomes', *Review of Educational Research* 53 (4) 519–569.

Male, J. and Thompson, C. (1985) *The Educational Implications of Disability*. London, RADAR.

Mann L. (1980) '94–142 ho!', *The Journal of Special Education* 14 (i) 2–3.

Marwick, A. (1968) *Britain in a Century of Total Wars: War, Peace and Social Change 1900–1967*. London, Bodley Head.

Maslow, A. H. (1943) 'A Theory of Human Motivation', *Psychology Review* 50 370–396.

May-Wilson, J. and Broadhead G. D. (1979) 'Integrating Special and Remedial Education', *Remedial Education* 14 (2) 85–90.

Mayo, E. (1933) *The Human Problems of Industrial Civilization*. New York, Macmillan.

McCall, C. (1980) 'Ways of Providing for Low Achievers in the Secondary School, Suggested advantages disadvantages and alternatives', *Educational Review*. Occasional Publications 7.

McKenzie, J. C. (1981) 'The Teaching of Geography for Children with Learning Difficulties', *Remedial Education* 16 (3) 57–60.

McNicholas, J. (1981) 'Life skills: a course for non-academic fourth and fifth years in a Comprehensive School', *Remedial Education* 16 (3) 125–129.

McNicholas, J. (1979) in Gains, C. and McNicholas, J. *Guidelines for the Future.* London, Longman.

McNiff, J. (1988) *Action Research. Principles and Practice.* London, Routledge.

Mepstead, J. (1988) 'Teachers' Attitudes', *Special Children* 17, January, p 14–15.

Melton, R. F. (1994) 'Competences in Perspective', *Educational Research* 36 285–294.

Midwinter, E. (1974) in Widlake, P. (1977).

Midwinter, E. (1980) *School and Society. The Evolution of English Education.* London, Routledge and Keegan Paul.

Miller, O. and Garner, M. (1996) 'Professional development to meet special educational needs', *British Journal of Special Education.* 23 (2) 70–77.

Ministry of Education (1963) *Half our Future. A Report of the Central Council for Education (England).* London, HMSO.

Ministry of Education (1945) *The Handicapped Pupil and The School Health Service Regulations. Statutory Rules and Orders No 1076.* London, HMSO.

Ministry of Education (1943) *White Paper on Educational Reconstruction.* London, HMSO.

Mintzberg, H. (1973) *The Nature of Managerial Work.* New York, Harper and Row.

Mintzberg, H. and Quinn, J. B. (1991) *The Strategy Process: Concepts, Contexts and Cases.* London, Prentice Hall.

Mittler, P. (1992) 'Educational Entitlement in the Nineties', *Support for Learning* 7 (4) 145–151.

Mittler, P. (1992) 'Presidential Address: National Association for Special Education', *Support for Learning* 7 (3) 145–151.

Moon, R. (1994) *A Guide to the National Curriculum.* Oxford, Oxford University Press.

Moore, J. (1990) 'Local Education Authority Restructuring under ERA, Meeting or Creating Special Needs', *Support for Learning* 6 (1) 16–21.

Moseley, D. (1980) *Special Provision for Reading.* Windsor, NFER.

Moyle, D. (1982) 'Recent Developments in Reading and their Effects on Remedial Education', *Remedial Education* 17 (4) 151–155.

Mitchell, D. R. (1996) 'The rules keep changing: Special Education in a reforming education system', *International Journal of Disability, Development and Education* 43 (1) 55–74.

Musgrove, P. W. (1968) *Society and Education Since 1800.* London, Methuen.

Nash, C. in Dyson, A. and Gains, C. (1993) *Special Education to the year 2000.* London, David Fulton.

National Association for Remedial Education (1990) *Curriculum Access for All. A Special Educational Needs Training Pack for Staff Development.* Stafford, NARE.

National Association for Remedial Education (1977) *Report on In Service Training*. Stafford, NARE.

National Association of Remedial Education (1979) *Guidelines No 2. The Role of the Remedial Teacher*. Stafford, NARE.

National Curriculum Council (1989c) *Curriculum Guidance (2) A Curriculum for All*. York, National Curriculum Council.

National Curriculum Council (1989a) *Implementing the National curriculum. Circular No 5*. York, National Curriculum Council.

National Curriculum Council (1989b) *A Curriculum for All: SEN in the National Curriculum*. York, National Curriculum Council.

National Curriculum Council (1993) *Special Needs and the National Curriculum: Opportunity and Challenge*. York, National Curriculum Council.

National Fund for Research into Crippling Diseases (1979) *Integrating the Disabled. Evidence to the Snowdon Working Party*. London, NFRCD.

National Association of Schoolmasters/Union of Women Teachers (1986) *Special Educational Needs in Mainstream Education. Policy Statement*. Birmingham NAS/UWT.

National Union of Teachers (1992) *NUT Survey on Pupil Exclusions. Information for LEAs*. London, NUT.

National Union of Teachers (1979) *Special Educational Needs. The NUT response to Warnock*. Rednal, NUT.

Network: DES/LAPP (1984) *Bulletin*, Autumn 1984.

Norwich, B. and Clowne, E. (1985) 'Training with a school focus', *British Journal of Special Education* 12 (4) 167–169.

Norwood Committee (1943) *The Curriculum and Examinations in Secondary Schools*. London, HMSO.

OFSTED (1996) *The Implementation of the Code of Practice, a report by OFSTED*. London, HMSO.

O'Grady, M. (1992) 'For Better, For Worse, in Sickness and in Health', *Times Educational Supplement*, 17 April, p 18.

O'Hanlon, C. (1993a) in Gains, C. and Dyson, A. (1993) *Special Education to the year 2000*. London, David Fulton.

O'Hanlon, C. (1993b) *Special Education Integration in Europe*. London, David Fulton.

Open University (1996) *Post Graduate Certificate in Education Course Guide*. Milton Keynes, Open University Press.

Palmer, J. (ed) (1973) *Special Education in the New Community Services*. Ferndale, Jones.

Parents in Partnership Conference (1987) *Times Educational Supplement*, 23 October, p 1.

Partridge, J. (1966) *Life in a Secondary Modern School*. London, Penguin.

Patrick, H., Bernbaum, G. and Reid, K. (1981) Unpublished Paper, presented at UCET Annual Conference, Oxford.

Peddiwell, J. A. (1939) *The Sabre Tooth Curriculum*. London, McGraw Hill.

Pedley, R. (1969) *The Comprehensive School*. London, Penguin.

Peter, M. (1989) *Special Education Forward Trends* 16 (1) 18.

Peters, M. (1985) *Teaching the Catching of Spelling*. London, Routledge and Keegan Paul.

Peters, R. S. (1967) *Ethics and Education*. London, Unwin.

Peters, T. J. and Waterman, R. H. (1982) *In Search of Excellence: Lessons from America's Best-Run Companies*. London, Harper and Row.

Phinn, G. (1983) 'A Team Teaching Approach to Educating a Secondary Remedial Class', *Remedial Education* 18 (3) 100–107.

Pickup, M. (1995) 'The Role of the special educational needs co-ordinator: developing policy and practice' in *Support for Learning* 10 (ii) 88–92.

Pijil, S. J. and Meijer, C. J. W. (1991) 'Does integration count for much? An analysis of practices in eight countries', *European Journal of Special Needs Education* 6 (2) 100–111.

Pike, N. 'Expenditure fear over special help' in *Times Educational Supplement*, 29 November 1996, p 3.

Popper, K. (1945) *The Open Society and its Enemies*. London, Routledge and Keegan Paul.

Pritchard, D. G. (1963) *Education and the Handicapped 1760–1960*. London, Methuen.

Pumfrey, P. D. (1973) in Palmer, J. (ed) *Special Education in the New Community Services*. Ferndale, Jones.

Ranson, S. (1990) *The Politics of Reorganising Schools*. London, Unwin Hyman.

Ranson, S. (1994) *Towards the Learning Society*. London, Cassell.

Raven, J. (1977) *Education Values and Society*. London, Lewis.

Reid, K. and Alaras, B. (1980) 'Differences between the Views of Teachers and Students to aspects of Sixth Form Organisation at Three Contrasting Comprehensive Schools in South Wales', *Educational Studies* 6 (3).

Reid, M. *et al* (1976) *Mixed Ability Teaching Problems and Possibilities*. Windsor, NFER.

Reynolds, D. and Sullivan, M. (1987) *The Comprehensive Experiment*. Barcombe, Falmer Press.

Reynolds, M. C., Wang, C. and Walberg, H. J. (1987) 'The necessary restructuring of special and regular education', *Exceptional Children* (53) 391–398.

Richmond, R. (1979) 'Warnock Found Wanting and Waiting', *Special Education Forward Trends* 6 (3) 8–10.

Riddell, S. and Brown, S. (1994) *Special Educational Needs Policy in the 1990's. Warnock in the Market Place*. London, Routledge.

Roberts, L. and Williams, I. (1980) 'Three Years at Pringle School', *Special Education Forward Trends* 7 (3) 24–26.

Robson, C., Sebba, J., Mittler, P. and Davies, G. *In Service Training and Special educational Needs*. Manchester, Manchester University Press.

Robson, C. and Wright, M. (1989) 'SEN: Towards a modular pattern of INSET', *Support for Learning* 4 (2) 83–89.

Roda, G. (1991) *What is Integration? Its merit and issues in Italy*. Unpublished paper, Humberside Annual Special Education Conference.

Rogers, T. J. G. (1973) *The Bosworth Postscript*. Desford, Bosworth College.

Rowan, P. (1988) *Times Educational Supplement*.

Rowe, M. C. (1973) in Palmer, J. (ed) *Special Education in the New Community Services*. Ferndale, Jones.

Russell, P. (1981) *Concern*. (49) 6.

Russell, P. (1990) 'The Education Reform Act. The Implications for SEN' in Flude, M. and Hahher, M. (eds) *The Educational Reform Act: its Origins and Implications*. London, Falmer Press.

Rutter, M. (1986) *Helping Troubled Children*. London, Penguin.

Rutter, M., Tizari, J. and Whitemore, K. (1975) *Education, Health and Behaviour*. London, Longman.

Sabatino, D. A. (1981) 'Are appropriate educational programmes operationally achievable under mandated promises of PL 94–142?', *The Journal of Special Education* 15 (i) 9–23.

Salmon, H. and Poster, C. D. (1988) 'The management of Special Educational Needs' in Poster, C. D. and Day, C. *Partnerships in Educational Management*. London, Routledge.

Sampson, O.and Pumfrey, P. D. (1970) 'A Study of Remedial Education at the Secondary Stage of Schooling', *Remedial Education* 5 (3) in Widlake, P. (1977) *Remedial Education: programmes and projects. A reader*. London, Longman.

Sampson, O. (1975) *Remedial Education*. London, Routledge and Keegan Paul.

Sayer, J. (1987) *Secondary Scools For All? Strategies for Special Needs*. London, Cassell.

Sayer, J. (1989) *Managing Schools*. London, Hodder and Stoughton.

Schein, E. H. (1985) *Organisational Culture and Leadership: A Dynamic View*. San Francisco, Jossey-Bass.

Schon, D. A. (1971) *Beyond the Stable State*. London, Temple Smith.

Schonell, F. J. and Wall, W. D. (1949) 'Remedial Education Centre', *Educational Review* 3–30.

Schonell, F. J. (1942) *Backwardness in Basic Subjects*. London, Oliver and Boyd.

Schools' Council (1970) *Crossed with Adversity. The Education of Socially Disadvantaged Children in Secondary Schools. Schools' Council Working*

Paper 27. London, Evans Methuen.

Schools Council (1968) *Enquiry 1*. London, Schools Council.

Schools Council (1971) *Slow learners in the Secondary School. Working Paper 15*. London, HMSO.

Scott, E. (1995) in Dyson, A. and Gains, C. (1995) 'The Role of the Special Needs Co-ordinator: Poisoned Chalice or Crock of Gold', *Support for Learning* 10 (2).

Sebba, J. and Robson, C. (1988) 'Evaluating short, school focussed INSET courses in special educational needs', *British Journal of Special Education* 15 (3) 111–115.

Segal, S. S. (1963) *Teaching Backward Pupils*. London, Evans.

Self, H., Benning, A., Marston, D. and Magnusson, D (1991) 'Cooperative teaching project: A model for students at risk', *Exceptional Children* 58 (1) 26–35.

Semmel, M. A., Abernathy, T. V., Butera, G. and Lesar, S. (1991) 'Teacher Perceptions of the Regular Education Initiative', *Children* 58 (1) 9–23.

Sewell, G. (1982) *Reshaping Remedial Education*. London, Croom Helm.

Shaw, B. (1983) *Comprehensive Schools: The Impossible Dream?* Oxford, Blackwell.

Shaw, L. (1990) *Each Belongs: Studies of Integration in Canada*. London, Centre for Studies on Integration in Education.

Sheldon, D. (1989) 'How was it for You? Pupils, Parents and Teachers: Perspectives on Integration', *British Journal of Special Education* 18 (3).

Simon, B. (1988) *Bending the Rules*. London, Lawrence and Wishart.

Simpson, J. (1993) 'Rethinking the role of the special needs coordinator: quality assurance' in Dyson, A. and Gains, C. *Rethinking Special Needs in Mainstream Schools: Towards the Year 2000*. London, David Fulton.

Sintra, C. (1981) in Swann, W. (ed) *The Practice of Special Education*. Oxford, Blackwell.

Slavin, R.E., Madden, N. A., Karweit, N. L., Dolan, L., Wasik, B. A., Shaw, A., Mainzer, K. L. and Haxby, B. (1991) 'Neverstreaming: prevention and early intervention as an alternative to special education', *Journal of Learning Disabilities* 24 (6) 373–378.

Solstis, J. F. (1980) *An introduction to an Analysis of Educational Concepts*. New York, Addison Wesley.

Smith, C. J. (ed) (1985) *New Directions in Remedial Education*. Lewis, Falmer.

Smith, J. G. (1985) *Business Strategy*. Oxford, Blackwell.

Spastics Society (1992) *A Hard Act to Follow*. London, Spastics Society.

Special Educational Needs Training Consortium (SENTC) (1996) *Professional Development to Meet Special Educational Needs Report to the Department for Education and Employment*. SENTC.

Spens, W. (Chairman) (1938) *Secondary Education*. London, HMSO.

Stainback, W. and Stainback, S. (1984) 'A rationale for the merger of special and regular education', *Exceptional Children* (51) 102–111.

Stainback, W. and Stainback, S. (eds) (1990) *Support Networks for Inclusive Schooling: interdependent Integrated Education*. Baltimore, Paul H Brookes.

Stakes, J. R. (1988) 'From the Remedial Department to Special Education. An Anatomy of Change Provision in a Comprehensive School', *School Organisation* 8 (1).

Stakes, J. R. (1985) *The process of Education and its effects on the Academically Less Successful Pupil in the Secondary School*. Unpublished MA (Ed) thesis, University of Durham.

Stakes, J. R. (1990) *The Warnock Report and its Effects on provision for Pupils with Special Educational Needs in Mainstream Schools*. Unpublished PhD thesis, University of Hull.

Stakes, J. R. (1996) *The Code in Practice, Some Preliminary Thoughts from Teachers*. Doncaster College, Occasional Papers.

Stakes, J. R and Hornby, G. (1996) 'Special Educational Needs: the National Curriculum' in Andrews, R. (ed) *Interpreting the New National Curriculum*. London, Middlesex University Press.

Stenhouse, L. (1975) *An Introduction to Curriculum Research and Development*. London, Heinemann.

Stewart, J. and Ranson, S. (1988) *Management in the Public Domain*. Local Government Training Board Paper, p 1–20.

Sumner, R. and Warburton, F. W. (1972) *Achievement in Secondary School. Attitudes, Personality and School Success*. London, Routledge and Keegan Paul.

Sutherland, G. (1981) in Swann, W. (ed) (1981) *The Practice of Special Education*. Oxford, Blackwell.

Swann, W. (1981) *The Practice of Special Education*. Oxford, Blackwell.

Swann, W. (1991) *Variations between LEAs and Levels of Segregation in Special schools (1982–1990): preliminary report*. London, Centre for Studies on Integration.

Swann, W. (1985) 'Is the integration of children with special needs happening? An analysis of recent statistics of pupils in special schools', *Oxford Review of Education*. 11 (1) 3–18.

Tansley, A. E. and Gulliford, R. (1960) *The education of the Slow Learning Child*. London, Routledge and Keegan Paul.

Tansley, P. and Pankhurst, J. (1981) *Children with Specific Learning Difficulties*. Windsor, NFER.

Taylor, F. W. (1911) *Principles of Scientific Management*. New York, Harper.

Taylor, W. (1963) *Life in a Secondary Modern School*. London, Faber.

Teacher Training Agency (1996) *Career Entry Profile for a Newly Qualified Secondary Teacher*. London TTA.

The University of London Institute of Education (1986) *The 1981 Education Act. Policy and Provision for Special Educational Needs. A report presented to the National Dissemination Conference.* London, University of London.

Thomas, D. (1982) *Teachers' Attitudes towards Integrating Educationally Sub-normal Children in Devon.* Melbourne, Flinders University Australia.

Thomas, D. (1988) 'The Dynamics of Teacher Opposition to Integration', *Remedial Education* 20 (2) 53–58.

Thomas, D. (1993) in Dyson, A. and Gains, C. (1993) *Special Education to the year 2000.* London, David Fulton.

Thomas, E. (1961) *The Handicapped School Leaver. Report of the Working Party Commissioned for the Re-habilitation of the Disabled.* Melbourne, Flinders University, South Australia.

Tice, W. (1979) 'Is anyone out there really listening?', *Education Unlimited* 1 (v) 30–31.

Times Educational Supplement (1996) 'Special needs Code proves hard to crack', 5 January.

Times Educational Supplement (1996) 'Unhappy verdict on vocational awards', June 14, p 8.

Tizard, J. (1949) 'Maladjusted Children and the Child Guidance Service', *London Educational Review* 2 (2) 22–37.

Tizard, J. (1978) 'Research in Special Education', *Special Education Forward Trends* 5 (3) 23–26.

Tomlinson, S. (1982) *A Sociology of Special Education.* London, Routledge and Keegan Paul.

Topping, K. (1975) 'An Evaluation of the Long term Effects of Remedial Teaching', *Remedial Education* 10 (1).

Torrington, D. and Weightman, J. (1989) *The Reality of School Management.* Oxford, Blackwell Educational.

Training and Development Lead Body (TDLB) (1994) *National Standards for Assessment and Verification.* London, HMSO.

Tredgold, A. F. (1910) *Mental Deficiency.* London, Baillière Tindall, Cox.

Tuckey, L. (1972) in Palmer, J. (ed) *Special Education in the New Community Services.* Ferndale, Jones.

University of London (undated) *Education of Backward Children.* London, London University Institute of Education.

Walters, B. (1994) *Management for Special Needs.* London, Cassell.

Wang, M. C., Reynolds, M. C. and Walberg, H. J. (1988) 'Integrating the children of the second system', *Phi Delta Kappa* (70) 248–251.

Wang, M. C. and Walberg, H. J. (1983) 'Adaptive instruction and classroom time', *American Educational Research* (20) 601–626.

Warnock, M. (1982) 'Children with Special Needs in Ordinary Schools: Integration Revisited', *Education Today* 32 (3).

Warnock, M. (1992) 'Special Case in Need of Reform', *The Observer*, 18 October, *also* BBC Panorama Programme 19 October 1992.

Warnock, M. (1993) in Vissar, J. and Upton, G. (eds) *Special Education in Britain after Warnock*. London, David Fulton.

Watkins, J. R. and Lewis, S. (1983) 'Examining Children who have Problems with Reading and Writing: a Case Study of CSE Biology', *Remedial Education* 18 (2) 59–63.

Watts, J. (1978) *The Countesthorpe Experience*. London, Unwin.

Webber, M. (1947) *The Theory of Social and Economic Organisations*. Translated A. M. Henderson and T. Parsons. Glencoe Ill, The Fress Press.

Webber, M. (1978) *Economy and Society*. Berkeley, University of California.

Webster, A. (1994) 'The new Code of practice for Children with SEN: implications for those working with hearing-impaired pupils', *Journal of the British Association for teachers of the Deaf* 18 (4) 97–108.

Weddell, K. (1988) *The 1981 Education Act. Policy and Provision for Special Educational Needs*. London, Cassell.

Weddell, K. (1988) 'The New Act: A Special Need for Vigilance', *British Journal of Special Education* 15 (3) 98–101.

Weedon, C. (1994) 'Learning Difficulties in Mathematics' in Riddell, S. and Brown, S. (eds) *Special Educational Needs Policy in the 1990s. Warnock in the Market Place*. London, Routledge.

Welton, J. (1989) 'Incrementalism to catastrophy theory: policy for children with special educational needs' in Roaf, C. and Bines, H. (eds) *Needs, Rights and Opportunities*. Lewis, Falmer Press.

Welton, J. and Evans, J. (1986) 'The Development and Implementation of Special Education Policy: Where did the 1981 Education Act fit in?', *Public Administration* 64 (7).

Welton, J., Weddell, K. and Vortays, G. (1982) 'Meeting Special Educational Needs: The 1981 Education Act and its Implications', *Bedford Way Papers* 12. London, Heinemann.

Weston, P. (1986) 'If Success has Many Faces: the Lower Attaining Pupils Programme', *Forum* 28 (3).

Westwood, P. (1975) *The Remedial Teacher's Handbook*. London, Oliver and Boyd.

Westwood, P. (1993) *Commonsense Methods with Pupils with Special Educational Needs*. London, Routledge.

Whayman, R. (1985) 'A Foundation Maths Scheme for Children with Learning Difficulties in the Secondary School', *Remedial Education* 19 (2) 179.

White, J. (1991) 'The Goals are the same ... are they?', *British Journal of Special Education* 18 (i) 25–26.

Widlake, P. (1977) *Remedial Education: Programmes and Projects. A Reader*. London, Longman.

Widlake, P. (1984) *How to Reach the Hard to Teach*. Milton Keynes, Open University Press.

Williams, K. (1969) 'The Role of the Remedial Department in a Comprehensive School', *Remedial Education* 4 (2) in Widlake, P. (1977).

Williams, R. (1958) *Culture and Society*. London, Chatto and Windus.

Willis, P. (1977) *Learning to Labour. How Working Class Kids Get Working Class Jobs*. Farnborough, Saxon House.

Wilson, M. D. (1985) *History for pupils with Learning Difficulties*. London, Hodder and Stoughton.

Wolfendale, S. (1993) *Assessing Special Educational Needs*. London, Cassell.

Woods, P. (1978) 'Negotiating the Demands of Schoolwork', *Journal of Curriculum Studies* 10 (4) 309–327.

Woodward, J. (1970) *Industrial Organisation: Behaviour and Control*. London, Oxford University Press.

Wragg, E. C. (1972) *An Introduction to Classroom Observation*. London, Routledge.

Yeager, P. (1979) 'Parents speak on the IEP', *The Directive Teacher* 2 (i) 13–14.

Young, M. F. D. (ed) (1971) *Knowledge and Control*. London, Collier Macmillan.

Zigler, E. and Hodapp, R. M. (1986) *Understanding Mental Retardation*. Cambridge, Cambridge University Press.

Author Index

General Index